INNOVATION MAKERS

INNOVATION MAKERS

HOW CAMPUS MAKERSPACES ARE EMPOWERING STUDENTS TO CHANGE THE WORLD

EMI MAKINO

NEW DEGREE PRESS

COPYRIGHT © 2020 EMI MAKINO

INNOVATION MAKERS

How campus makerspaces are empowering students to change the world

ISBN   978-1-63676-546-4   *Paperback*

           978-1-63676-105-3   *Kindle Ebook*

           978-1-63676-106-0   *Ebook*

For Joseph A. Maciariello

CONTENTS

INTRODUCTION

When you come to a fork in the road, take it!

—YOGI BERRA

When Doris Drucker, my mentor, invited me to lunch, she sometimes talked about Yogi Berra. I had been awarded a fellowship in her name when my family and I relocated from Tokyo to Los Angeles so I could pursue an MBA degree. Doris would occasionally pick me up in her black Toyota Camry and drive me to a Thai restaurant in La Verne, fifteen minutes away from Claremont Graduate University where I studied. She was a few years shy of her hundredth birthday.

More than half a century before in the 1950s and '60s, she lived in Montclair, New Jersey, with her husband Peter, the famous management philosopher and consultant. Peter was teaching at New York University. Doris felt out of place in Montclair, which she described as a "conformist society of an upper-class suburb."[1]

---

1   Doris Drucker, *Invent Radium or I'll Pull Your Hair* (Chicago: University of Chicago Press, 2004), 187.

The baseball player was the most famous person in town, yet he was also known for his unpretentiousness.[2] "I think the only person in Montclair with whom (Peter) had any affinity and whom he liked to meet was Yogi Berra,"[3] she recalled in her memoir.

The Druckers and Berra were neighbors, and they became good friends. During our conversations, Doris would fondly recall how he used to tell them, "When you come to a fork in the road, take it!"

Each time I heard this story, I would smile nervously. I honestly could not grasp the meaning of this particular Yogiism. "Which fork does he mean we should take?" I would think, missing the point entirely.

It took me years to appreciate why Doris, an entrepreneur, loved those words so much. It didn't matter which fork we took. The point was to take it. It was similar to one of the cardinal rules of entrepreneurship: Action trumps everything. I used to think that conceiving an idea, analyzing it, strategizing about its potential, and planning for it, was at the heart of creating startups. I was wrong. Entrepreneurship is initiated and sustained only through action and, by taking the forks.

Doris would have loved and appreciated the makerspace Hongo Tech Garage, an oasis and secret base for students aspiring to change the world. It is where students of the University of Tokyo are literally pumping out one innovation after another every spring and summer. Students who participate in the intensive incubation program offered there

---

2   Kate Zernike, "A New Jersey Township Mourns Yogi Berra, Its Civic Treasure," *New York Times*, September 23, 2015.

3   Drucker, *Invent Radium*, 187.

live by the mantra "Deploy or Die!" borrowed from Joi Ito, former director of MIT Media Lab.

Empowered by advances in digital fabrication tools, changing the world is no longer an ideal; it is a reality waiting to be seized by those who live by Berra's words. The machines at the Garage are nothing fancy: standard 3-D printers, a laser cutter, a CNC milling machine, and some hand tools. But they are functional, free, and accessible to students.

Plus, there are deadlines to meet. In just one week, teams must have a prototype ready for demonstration or risk being asked to leave. The students featured in this book give us a glimpse of the disruption that awaits higher education, a future where students play a central role in the production of innovation, new knowledge, and scientific contributions.

Take the experience of Masaki Takeuchi, a master's student in electrical engineering. He chose the University of Tokyo for his graduate studies because he wanted to dramatically improve the lives of people who had lost their voices due to disease. He wasn't accepted to the lab of his choice, however. So, he took a fork in the road. He signed up for the Summer Founders Program (SFP) at the Garage, which quietly opened its doors in 2016.

Innovation means more than invention. It is about creating new value where none existed before. Research outcomes must be tailored to fit a specific context in which a particular set of users see value. Commercializing the invention can sometimes be more challenging than the research and development. This is where scientists often stumble.

Masaki started from the user's perspective, not the technology.[4] A few weeks before SFP's application deadline, he

____

4   *Throughout this book, I will refer to students by their first names.*

learned about the plight of laryngectomees—people who have had their voice boxes removed for medical reasons. The current products on the market were unremarkable. Why not apply machine-learning techniques to enable these patients to regain their natural voices?

He knew that 3-D printers would be essential for making prototypes. With one click on a computer screen, these desktop machines melt a plastic rod into a nozzle that digitally injects the material onto a board in layers to create a three-dimensional object like the electrolarynx device Masaki wanted to develop. However, he lacked the necessary engineering and technical skills. He applied to SFP anyway and was accepted on the strength of his idea.

On the first day of the program, he met a few students who were very strong in 3-D modeling and engineering. They didn't have a problem to solve though. So, they decided there and then to join forces.

Within a few weeks, Masaki's team was already testing a crude but working prototype with real users. By combining artificial intelligence (AI) and biomimicry, they achieved in months what had not been done in decades: a significant upgrade in electrolarynx technology. Conventional electrolarynx devices sound guttural and monotonic, evoking images of Darth Vader. Their product, called Syrinx, needs only a tiny voice sample to be taken before surgery in order to reproduce the exact vibration patterns of the patient to generate more natural-sounding voices.

The following year in late May, when many parts of the world were under lockdown from COVID-19, including Tokyo, I received a cryptic Facebook message from Katsufumi Matsui, my research collaborator who currently runs the Garage.

"So close…"

A link to an article on Microsoft's website followed.

Apparently, Masaki's team had entered Microsoft's Imagine Cup for students, a global competition for innovations that tackle the toughest problems of the world. Dubbed the "Olympics of student technology competitions," more than two million students have competed over the past eighteen years to "build what matters" for a chance to win one hundred thousand US dollars in cash and a mentoring session with Microsoft's CEO.

In the fall of 2019, thousands of students registered for the competition, with six teams advancing to the world championship.[5] Team Syrinx was one of them. Due to COVID-19, the teams pitched their projects virtually, and the winner had just been announced.

Syrinx team members wearing the electrolarynx they developed
(Masaki Takeuchi is second from the right)

---

5   "2020 World Finalists," on *Imagine Cup's website*, accessed September 2, 2020.

Syrinx had placed second. I quickly messaged back.

"So close!!!! But second place might actually help bear real fruit."

I said this because it is an open secret that the teams that lose in these competitions often end up becoming successful ventures. While there is no empirical research to back this claim, I've heard this many times from organizers of events like Startup Weekend. Failure can be a tremendous source of motivation.[6]

This book explores how student-led innovations are no longer random, lucky events that happen only when the stars align. Universities are discovering that when students are given access to digital maker technologies through dedicated makerspaces, along with structured educational programs, they can generate innovations with real impact.

For this book, I will use the word "makerspace" instead of "maker space" with the expectation that use of the former will eventually become mainstream. Robert Perhamus, who created one in the Claremont area, informed me that that the use of the word "makerspace" without a space increased rapidly since 2009, according to a Google Trends search in September 2020. Usage dipped slightly during the pandemic, but the trend line appeared to be heading back up.

The students featured in this book are more agile and action-oriented than professional scientists and researchers at universities who are paid to innovate. They also have access to expensive equipment and research infrastructure. Facebook was a student innovation born out of a dorm room

---

6 Yasuhiro Yamakawa, Mike W. Peng, and David L. Deeds, "Rising from the Ashes: Cognitive Determinants of Venture Growth after Entrepreneurial Failure," *Entrepreneurship Theory and Practice* 39, no. 2 (2015).

made possible by "borrowing" campus servers for its website. Students, therefore, are well-positioned to commercialize technology products quickly and effectively.

Makerspaces on-and off-campus enable students to do more. They can now develop novel physical products and innovations, which are arguably more difficult than information-and software-based services.

My first encounter with such a space was in 2014. I vividly recall being totally blown away when I was given a guided tour of TechShop, a commercial operation near San José State University. The so-called "maker movement" was in full throttle there.

For the uninitiated like myself, the digital machines there thrust me into the future. I had seen a 3-D printer before, but never a UV printer capable of applying special ink in full color onto virtually any surface whether it be plastic, rubber, or glass. A huge water jet cutter squirted out water at such high pressure it sliced through metal and granite with precision.

The machines were both inspiring and empowering. Local restaurateurs in the Bay Area were designing and fabricating everything from signage to the decorations and furnishings for the interior design of their restaurants. They were liberated from contractors who would charge exorbitant amounts of money and still get it wrong. I also heard the story of Embrace Innovations, founded by Stanford University students, who developed a heated blanket for premature babies needing incubators in rural communities with no running electricity. Their invention had already saved over two hundred thousand babies by 2017.[7]

---

7 Gleb Savich, "Embrace Infant Warmers Help Save Lives of Preterm Babies in Developing Countries," *Medium.com*, December 8, 2017.

What I was seeing was not science fiction. Making predictions in human affairs is pointless, according to Peter Drucker. "But it is possible and fruitful to identify major events that have already happened, irrevocably, and that therefore will have predictable effects in the next decade or two. It is possible, in other words, to identify and prepare for the future *that has already happened*." [8]

Internet guru Chris Anderson, former editor-in-chief of *WIRED* magazine, is convinced that the maker movement will easily surpass the Web movement of the late '90s and early 2000s in terms of impact.[9] That movement was driven by bits, the units of information. For all our fascination with the virtual world of the Internet though, we still live firmly grounded in a world of atoms.

"To put a ballpark figure on it, the digital economy, broadly defined, represents 20 trillion dollars of revenues, according to Citibank and Oxford Economics. The economy beyond the Web, by the same estimate, is about 130 trillion dollars. In short, the world of atoms is at least five times larger than the world of bits," wrote Anderson in his book *Makers*. [10]

Digital tools have made it possible for people without much training or money to make highly customized, commercial-grade products at a small scale. Anderson calls this the democratization of manufacturing. "Just as the Web democratized innovation in bits, a new class of 'rapid prototyping' technologies, from 3-D printers to laser cutters, is

---

8   Peter F. Drucker, "The Future That Has Already Happened," *Harvard Business Review*, September-October, 1997.

9   Chris Anderson, *Makers: The New Industrial Revolution* (Crown Books, 2012), Kindle.

10   Anderson, *Makers*, 14.

democratizing innovation in atoms. You think the last two decades were amazing? Just wait."[11]

I had front-row seats during the Web Revolution. I happened to be in the right place at the right time—New York City in the mid-'90s—when I had the opportunity to interview and write about some of the world's greatest entrepreneurs and executives in the United States, including Jeff Bezos and Eric Schmidt. It was dazzling. From my desk on the twenty-fifth floor of a high-rise office tower in midtown Manhattan, I watched in awe as the commercial Internet literally unfolded on my computer.

The by-lined articles I wrote on e-commerce and software appeared often and with prominence in the various Japanese newspapers published by Nikkei. Its flagship, *The Nikkei*, was a powerhouse, with a circulation of nearly three million at the time.[12] Being in New York, it was hard to see the impact of my stories. But a colleague in Tokyo told me that my article on the emergence of free phone calls using the Internet had made a stir in our national parliament. Apparently, a Diet member waved a copy of the article during a parliamentary session, demanding the government to take action against the technologies that were poised to disrupt the telecom industry.

Unfortunately, corporate Japan, policy makers, and administrators were slow to respond to digital transformation. Decades of stagnation followed. And now, Japan once again is at a fork in the road. This time, the stakes may be

---

11   Anderson, *Makers*, 14.

12   Miyateu, "日本経済新聞の新聞発行部数推移を50年間分まとめてみた【1970年から2020年】(50 Years Worth of Nikkei Shimbun Circulation Data [1970-2020])," 新聞についてまとめてみた, May 17, 2020.

even higher. If Anderson is right, digital fabrication technologies may eventually shatter and shutter the economic bedrock of Japan: its giant manufacturing industry.

Scholars have yet to figure out the full implications of digital manufacturing.[13] There are telltale signs, though, like the incredible growth in the "additive manufacturing" or 3-D printing market. Valuates Reports estimated global market size in 2019 was 6.4 billion US dollars. The market would grow at a compounded annual growth rate of 31.4 percent, topping 44 billion US dollars by 2026.

Driving the growth is the versatility of 3-D printing. It can be used for applications in a wide range of products including industrial devices, automobiles, houses, medical and dental devices, and even personalized food.[14]

The pandemic was a startling reminder that we cannot live on Netflix alone. Giant Japanese multinationals have been hit particularly hard by the disruptions in their global supply chains. Japan's gross domestic product (GDP) plunged in the April-June quarter in 2020, recording the biggest postwar contraction ever. Japan's economy shrank by 27.8 percent on an annualized basis.[15]

While this is frightening, there is a silver lining. The "third industrial revolution" Anderson talked about in his book *Makers* may accelerate. Anderson expects "a new kind

---

13   Danfang Chen et al., "Direct Digital Manufacturing: Definition, Evolution, and Sustainability," *Journal of Cleaner Production* 107 (2015).

14   Valuates Reports, "3D Printing (Additive Manufacturing) Market Size is Expected to Reach USD 44520 Million By 2026 at a CAGR 31.4%," *PR Newswire*, March 16, 2020.

15   Mitsuru Obe, "Japan GDP Contracts Annualized 27.8% in April-June," *Nikkei Asian Review*, August 17, 2020.

of manufacturing economy" to take hold, one "shaped more like the Web itself: bottom-up, broadly distributed, and highly entrepreneurial."[16]

Digital natives like Masaki are the heroes of the emerging new paradigm. I have been a supporter and cheerleader of the startup ecosystem in Japan since my days as a business reporter more than twenty years ago. Yet during all this time, early-stage entrepreneurial activity in Japan has constantly been staggeringly low compared to other developed nations.[17]

Frustrated, I decided to go back to school. I was already in my late thirties, and I was desperate to figure out why Japan just couldn't seem to get it right when it came to startups. I studied for my MBA and PhD, but I left with more questions than answers.

It has been through my struggles in teaching, that I have finally been able to identify some possible solutions. For over seven years now, I have immersed myself in entrepreneurship education at various universities in Japan. My colleagues have pointed me to effective ways for developing entrepreneurs who can deal with uncertainty. These teaching methods are grounded in solid, theoretical, and empirical research. In addition, best practices from successful accelerators and incubators have given us additional processes and frameworks for designing programs with impact.

This book is unique in that it examines the critical importance of *making things* in educating entrepreneurs. The physical act of creation is an inherent need and skill in all humans.

---

16   Anderson, *Makers*, 24.

17   Mizuho Information and Research Institute, 平成３０年度創業・起業支援事業（起業家精神に関する調査）*(FY2018 Report on Entrepreneurial Spirit Survey)*, (Tokyo: METI, March 2019).

The premise of this book is that it is also at the heart of entrepreneurship and innovation.

Producing things has never been easier. All it takes is downloading a digital file, tweaking it a little, and then sending it to a machine to do the work of cutting, carving, drilling, molding, dying, or whatever technique is called for. And voila, like magic, one can create something that looks professional.

Higher education is at the eye of the turbulent storm that is brewing amidst the dramatic changes occurring in manufacturing. Makerspaces embedded in the university ecosystem will become important drivers for commercializing technologies. Best practices from various campuses suggest that students can really change the world if institutions empower them with the space, tools, funding, and most importantly, structured programs.

Students will increasingly take a more active role in the production of knowledge, a role previously reserved exclusively for faculty. How higher education institutions recognize and embrace the coming transformation will determine their position in the emerging new world order, representing both an opportunity and a threat.

This book attempts to show that when effective, co-curricular programming is integrated into makerspaces at universities, magical things happen. I hope it will serve as a guide for educators and students who already have access to, or are thinking of establishing, makerspaces on campus.

It will also introduce readers interested in starting their own enterprises to the science behind innovation and entrepreneurship. The theories and methods culled from research and practice will help improve the odds of success by learning to act and make decisions like an expert entrepreneur.

I was compelled to write this book because the students I've met have been a constant source of energy and inspiration for me. Their curiosity, sense of purpose, and passion, when combined with a playful approach to science and technology, are enabling them to generate wildly original products and services with astonishing speed. I hope that their efforts will encourage more people to embrace the maker movement, see the fork, and take it.

PART I

HOW WE GOT HERE

CHAPTER 1

THE INNOVATION REVOLUTION

The biggest transformation is not in the way things are done, but in who's doing it.

—CHRIS ANDERSON

I bought my first book on Amazon.com on May 3, 1996. According to my order history, it was *Back Trouble: A New Approach to Prevention and Recovery*, a book about a specialized physical therapy technique published in 1987.

It was two years after I had graduated from Columbia University's journalism school. I was living in a small studio apartment in New York City near the Flatiron building, thousands of miles away from my home in Japan.

It was an amazing time to be in the United States. In 1993, when I was still in school, the world's first Internet browser, Mozilla, was released. I had taken a course on computer-assisted reporting taught by Steve Ross. We learned how to connect to databases via Telnet, then download files to analyze demographic and environmental data using spreadsheets. Everything was text-based and in green, since green-on-black was standard for computer displays on campus at the time.

Mozilla was revolutionary because its interface was graphical. Suddenly, we were liberated from typing text commands to connect to other computers. The World Wide Web emerged, and the Internet became something we could *browse*.

A flyer in my J-School mailbox led me to the New York bureau of Japan's largest business daily, *The Nikkei*. I was hired to report and write about business and the financial markets.

I wanted to apply what I had learned from Ross' course. So, I convinced my editors I needed a desktop PC and a modem connected to the Internet. My connection was over copper telephone wires with speeds of up to 9600 kilobits per second. Modems at the office were still rare, and very few people had access to the Internet.

Before the Web, I felt like an alien with no command of the language and conventions of using computer services. The Internet was different now. I could sense how our lives would be forever transformed.

From a news perspective, this would be one of the most important breaking stories of the '90s, and I was eager to cover the new frontier.

I was lucky. The more senior reporters at *The Nikkei* were too busy covering news about large, established companies like Toyota and IBM. No one had the time to write about the innovative technologies and startups that were changing the world.

I was more than happy to fill the void. From my desk at our bureau on the twenty-fourth floor of a high-rise office building in midtown Manhattan, I watched in awe as the Internet rapidly developed into a paradigm-shifting platform for business and commerce, literally at my fingertips.

"You should check this site out," suggested a reporting assistant, Hashimoto-san. He loved the Internet even more than I did, and he also knew I was always on the lookout for the coolest new websites. He had discovered Amazon.com, a virtual bookstore.

The site was simple. "One million titles. Consistently low prices." The only graphic on the home page was a light blue logo in the upper left-hand corner depicting the letter A with a river running through it. "Interesting," I thought.

I tried ordering a book that might help me in my quiet fight against repetitive stress injuries (RSI). Typing on deadline for more than fourteen hours a day for two years had taken a toll. My body was in shambles. My hands, wrists, elbows, shoulders, and upper back were sore all the time. I kept dropping my keys while opening my apartment door; my grip was too weak. It was painful to lift my arms and wash my hair. The water from the shower hurt the back of my hands.

My physical therapist had mentioned the Alexander Technique as a possibility for alleviating the symptoms from my RSI. I walked over to a giant Barnes & Noble bookstore that was a few blocks away. Despite the hundreds of books on the shelves, I could find none about the Alexander Technique. The topic was too arcane and specialized. So, I could hardly contain my excitement when *Back Trouble* actually arrived from Amazon.

Fast forward twenty-five years to today. What felt revolutionary a generation ago is downright ordinary now. *Everyone* seems to shop on Amazon, especially during the pandemic. But if thought leaders like Chris Anderson are right, then the rise of the World Wide Web is just an opening act to the main show, an appetizer to the main course.

Anderson is the former editor-in-chief of *WIRED* magazine, the publication that has chronicled the digital revolution. He has written books like *The Long Tail* and *Free*, which explained the implications of the Internet regarding how we do business. In 2010, he wrote an influential article on Wired.com that predicted the real revolution was only just beginning.

Transformative change happens when industries democratize, when they're ripped from the sole domain of companies, governments, and other institutions and handed over to regular folks. The Internet democratized publishing, broadcasting, and communications, and the consequence was a massive increase in the range of both participation and participants in everything digital—the long tail of bits. Now the same is happening to manufacturing—the long tail of things.[18]

The world of bits is but a fraction of the world of atoms, "also known as the Real World of Places and Stuff" according to Anderson. "Peer production, open source, crowdsourcing, user-generated content—all these digital trends have begun to play out in the world of atoms, too. The Web was just the proof of concept. Now the revolution hits the real world," he declared.[19]

---

18   Chris Anderson, "In the Next Industrial Revolution, Atoms Are the New Bits," *Wired.com*, January 25, 2010.

19   Anderson, "Atoms Are the New Bits."

In the twentieth century, inventors typically did not own the means of production. This was the case for Anderson's grandfather, Fred Hauser, whose various inventions were commercialized by others. Hauser worked in Hollywood as an engineer in recording technology. He liked to tinker and invent machines. He converted his garage into a workshop, where he developed and patented an automatic sprinkler system.

He could not get to market without a manufacturer, however. Herein lies the limitations of an inventor in the twentieth century. As Karl Marx observed, "The class which has the means of material production at its disposal, has control at the same time over the means of mental production, so that thereby, generally speaking, the ideas of those who lack the means of mental production are subject to it."[20] In other words, in a capitalist society, power belongs to those who control capital—money, land, labor, resources, etcetera.

Hauser persuaded a company to license his technology, and he received royalties for several decades until his patent ran out. But this was "a one-in-a-thousand success story," and was the only commercial hit for Hauser, who held twenty-six patents for other devices.[21]

The twenty-first century is different. First, society has transformed into one in which knowledge is a significant source of capital.[22] Second, far less capital is required for

---

20   Karl Marx, "German Ideology, 1845" *Karl Marx Quotes*, accessed September 7, 2020.

21   Chris Anderson, *Makers: The New Industrial Revolution* (New York: Crown Business, 2014), 6, Kindle.

22   Peter F. Drucker, *Post-Capitalist Society* (New York: HarperBusiness, 1993), Kindle.

manufacturing, research, and development thanks to digital technologies.

Consequently, micro-entrepreneurs can play hardball against the captains of industry. The convergence of cheap but powerful fabrication tools, programmable micro-controller boards like Arduino, opensource platforms like Github, and marketplaces like Etsy are leveling the playing field. Anderson called this transformation the maker movement.

I caught a glimpse of the new industrial revolution when I visited the Bay Area shortly into my first year of teaching entrepreneurship and management. I had given up journalism in the early 2000s; the typing injuries never completely healed.

Looking to build a career compatible with raising three children, I stumbled into the world of academia. With a PhD in hand, I accepted a teaching position at a prestigious research university in southern Japan called Kyushu University.

In February 2014, I reached out to Mark Hatch, who was then the CEO of TechShop, one of the world's first commercial chains of makerspaces. I had just finished reading his book, *The Maker Movement Manifesto*, which told the story of how TechShop was empowering a new generation of entrepreneurs to innovate. I e-mailed him that I would be in San Jose in mid-February accompanying graduate students I taught in the molecular systems device course. I wanted to visit TechShop and discuss what it would take to create makerspaces in Japan.

I had met Hatch at the Drucker School in my second year of my MBA there in 2009. He was an alum of the school and had come to campus to celebrate Peter Drucker's hundredth birthday. Drucker was a management consultant and prolific author "whose writings contributed to the philosophical and practical foundations of the modern business corporation."[23] He died in 2005.

Hatch told me that he had just joined a startup in Silicon Valley called TechShop, "a gym for geeks." I had never heard of CNC routers, nor had I even seen a 3-D printer. He described how TechShop members could access cutting-edge digital production machinery for a fixed monthly subscription fee, similar to an exercise club.

I had to wait five years, but I finally found myself walking through the doors of a makerspace. TechShop San Jose was located a few blocks from San José State University, where our students were spending four intense weeks studying English. They were also learning a little bit about entrepreneurship through visits to technology companies and startups in the Silicon Valley area.

TechShop was far beyond what I had imagined. The main shop floor was airy and bright. Areas for working with wood and metal were separated but still entirely visible. The largest and most expensive machine at the San Jose location could precision cut stone and glass using water.

While the machines were impressive, something else stood out: the variety of sewing and embroidery machines. In Japan, makerspaces called FabLabs (short for fabrication labs) were popping up all over the country. These spaces were smaller, but they still attracted many makers, mostly engineers. Machines for working with textiles were rarely part of the equipment portfolio. The core user base was predominantly male.

---

23   *Encyclopaedia Britannica Online*, s.v. "Peter F. Drucker: American Economist and Author," accessed September 7, 2020.

The members of TechShop also tilted toward men, but the presence of sewing machines made the place less intimidating for women. This attracted users not often associated with digital fabrication; for example, drama and theater types who came to make props, masks, and costumes for plays. Restaurateurs also regularly hung out at TechShop to create intricate displays, woodworking, and furnishings. Fun creations by members were on display, including a *Star Wars* lightsaber that actually worked.

I loved the place. It reminded me of the joy of making things for the sake of making things. It also had an entrepreneurial atmosphere. Many members were not just hobbyists; they were entrepreneurs. In fact, TechShop was instrumental for getting the mobile payment company Square off the ground. Jim McKelvey and his friend Jack Dorsey, founder of Twitter, pitched their idea for a smartphone app for credit card purchases to venture capitalists and initially "got absolutely nowhere."[24]

They needed a prototype. McKelvey went to TechShop in Menlo Park, became a member, "took a couple of classes, and in a matter of months had gone through three full generations of prototypes."[25] With a fully functional prototype in hand, the two raised 10 million dollars in Series A funding.

Hatch arranged for me to talk to the founder of TechShop, Jim Newton. With the help of "a group of diehard maker enthusiasts," opened the first TechShop in 2006 in the heart

---

24   Mark Hatch, *The Maker Movement Manifesto: Rules for Innovation in the New World of Crafters, Hackers, and Tinkerers* (New York: McGraw-Hill Education, 2013), 132, Kindle.

25   Hatch, *Manifesto*, 132.

of Silicon Valley. [26] Anyone over sixteen can be a member, with access to the "most powerful and easy-to-use machines the world has ever seen."[27]

"What makes TechShop so special?" I asked Newton.

"The community and serendipity," he answered.

He then told me the story of some Stanford students who began using TechShop to continue working on a project they had started at the d.school. Stanford's d.school is a famous interdisciplinary program where people from all over the university come to learn how to "use design to develop their own creative potential."[28] Access to the digital fabrication equipment on-site is included, but only while they are taking courses.

As part of the course, Design for Extreme Affordability, Jane Chen and her team were challenged to develop an incubator that could be provided for 1 percent of what one normally costs.[29]

Premature babies must be kept warm in an incubator to survive outside their mother's womb. Many rural communities in Africa and other developing areas do not have stable, running electricity, however.

As a result, babies die. Jane and her teammates tried to imagine an alternative solution that would not require constant electricity.

Their answer: a heated blanket that could be wrapped around the baby. In order to keep temperatures at a constant thirty-seven degrees Celsius, the blanket required some kind

---

26   Hatch, *Manifesto*, 3.

27   Hatch, *Manifesto*, 4.

28   "Stanford d.School," Stanford University, accessed August 29, 2020.

29   "Embrace," on Design for Extreme Affordability website, Stanford University, accessed August 29, 2020.

of power source. Unfortunately, time ran out. The team could not come up with a viable solution during the course.

They lost access to the equipment on campus they were using for prototyping. So, they turned to TechShop. According to Newton, it was there that one of the team members fell into a conversation with a chemical engineer. "Why don't you try chemistry?" Serendipity. This advice contributed to the technological breakthrough they needed.

The warmer uses phase-change material (PCM) made of a proprietary wax-like substance that can be reheated by immersing the warmer in boiling water. PCMs take advantage of heat released when a substance changes from solid to liquid, or vice versa.

The solution is decidedly low-tech, but highly effective. The final product looks like a tiny, blue sleeping bag and is currently priced at less than one hundred dollars. That compares to the twenty thousand-dollar price tag of an incubator.

What began as a student project has resulted in an innovation that has saved hundreds of thousands of babies, including Ayesha, who weighed only 1.1 kilograms at birth.

"Her father and mother lost their first two babies due to lack of proper medical care. They saved every penny they had so that their third child could be born in a city hospital, a four-hour walk from their village. Ayesha had a very low chance of survival and was kept in an incubator under observation for ten days. However, as her parents' savings ran out, it was not possible to extend her stay in the NICU. It was at that point that Ayesha was placed in the Embrace infant warmer for thermal support. After about a month, she gained sufficient weight and was able to go home."[30]

---

30   "About Us," on Embrace Innovations website, accessed August 29, 2020.

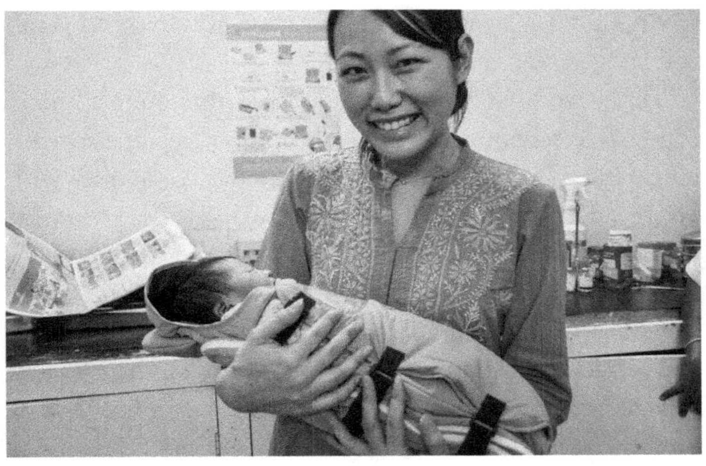

Jane Chen holding a baby in an Embrace infant warmer

"Healthtech with Heart." The Embrace Innovations website features a photo of Chen with Barack Obama. The technology Chen and her team applied was nothing fancy. But with passion, ingenuity, and persistence, they have saved three hundred thousand babies and counting. [31]

Student-driven innovations like the Embrace infant warmer are on the rise as more universities incorporate makerspaces into their entrepreneurship education offerings. As Anderson points out, what matters is not *how* the new maker technologies are changing the way things are done, or even *where*. It is about *who* is doing the transformation.

Social upheavals are often led by the younger generation. *National Geographic* magazine identified five movements fueled by young activists in recent history, including the

---

31 "About Us," Embrace Innovations.

Civil Rights Movement, Tiananmen Square, and Arab Spring. [32]

In the world of business, the transformation to a knowledge-based economy has enabled young entrepreneurs with no capital to speak of to topple blue-chip companies with unprecedented speed. In less than two decades, Amazon, Facebook, and Google (now Alphabet Inc.) are among the biggest companies in the world, overtaking Walt Disney, General Electric, and Toyota by market cap. Uber, Airbnb, and Netflix have followed and are bulldozing industries that used to be capital-intensive and had high barriers of entry.

More recently, Elon Musk has applied startup methods to research-intensive businesses with stunning results. He is simultaneously conquering the automobile, energy, and defense industries. His company, SpaceX, has literally disrupted the world of rocket science, something that was unthinkable in an industrial economy.

The pace of scientific innovations may accelerate as more and more students enter the fray. Hard-core research and development used to be out of reach for students, due to the high costs of equipment and the specialized skills necessary to use them. The democratization of manufacturing is changing these assumptions.

The golden combination of entrepreneurship programs and makerspaces in a research university setting may be a key source of innovations in the twenty-first century. In this scenario, students, not faculty, are the major players. At least, that was my hunch. The question in my mind as I left TechShop San Jose: Can this happen in Japan?

---

32   Erin Blakemore, "Youth in Revolt: Five Powerful Movements Fueled by Young Activists," *National Geographic.com*, March 23, 2018.

CHAPTER 2

THE CASE FOR CAMPUS MAKERSPACES

The day I e-mailed TechShop's Mark Hatch about my upcoming visit to the Bay Area, something magical happened right outside my building. As usual, I could hear the loud whir of jet engines. Kyushu University's Hakozaki campus was just five kilometers away from Fukuoka Airport, a major international gateway. Commercial planes would descend toward the skyline as they made their approach to the runway.

Students and faculty put up with the noise for years. Not for much longer though. In the age of nanodevices, the sonic waves wreaked havoc on highly sensitive machines and equipment. The decision was made to move the campus to the western fringes of Fukuoka City. Nearly all of the buildings would be demolished, including the one that housed the Robert T. Huang Entrepreneurship Center (QREC) where I had an office. But that February, the move was still a few years away.

It was a beautiful winter day; crisp air and blue skies. Cold.

I was working at my desk when all of a sudden, I could hear loud voices from the northwestern side of the building. They were outside. They seemed to be chanting very loudly. Shouting actually. Probably students. Curious, I peered out of my second-floor window.

What I saw was breathtaking: an enormous, wooden contraption, about two meters high and perhaps six meters long, shaped rather like a gigantic megaphone. Looking down, it seemed like a frame of huge Popsicle sticks connected with wooden panels. What stunned me, though, was not the size. The contraption was *moving*. It was turning around and around in time with the counting.

I had to see what was going on. I raced down the stairs and stepped outside. I counted maybe eight students. A few of them were in workwear, clothes more fitting for a shop floor than for taking classes. Two students were clearly out of breath, huffing and puffing as they pushed against the ends of the contraption to make it rotate in a steady rhythm. "One, two, three, four!" It was quite a feat to watch.

The machine stopped. I could see some handwriting on the whiteboard attached to one side.

WTDP Novel Revolving Type Wind Tunnel.
2nd Performance Test. February 5, 2014. 13:00~
Weather: Fair. Temperature: 8.2 Celsius.
Pressure: 1022 hPa. Natural wind: Max 1.6m/sec.

I glanced toward the bottom and noticed the credits to the special sponsors: QREC and Shin Nippon Feather Core Co.

Since 1987, QREC has been sponsoring student-initiated projects as part of its Challenge and Creation program, or C&C. Every spring, QREC selected eight student teams which were awarded five thousand dollars each to spend on a project they executed during the academic year, ending in March. The Wind Tunnel project was one of them.

I had joined the faculty of Kyushu University in April 2013. QREC was one of two centers I worked for. I recalled listening to over a dozen student pitches for the C&C program shortly after I arrived at QREC. That was May. I was blown away by the fact that in just nine months, the students had built such an enormous prototype, starting literally from nothing.

The students were having a grand time. Lots of laughing. High on adrenaline. It was clear who was in charge: a lanky, Western-looking guy with glasses and curly brown hair. I could hear no accent in his Japanese, however. Joshua Lawn, I later learned, was born and raised in Nagasaki. His father is from New Zealand, his mother from Japan. Japanese is his native language.

Joshua was captivated by wind power turbines. During high school, he spent many hours learning about fluid dynamics from a researcher at Nagasaki University. The Japan Science and Technology Agency (JST) had a special program that matched aspiring scientists like him with university faculty. Joshua had been chosen for three years in a row. This was how he came up with the initial idea of building a testing machine to measure how small wind turbines actually performed when generating power.

I approached him to ask some questions.

"These testing machines would have to be much bigger to accomplish what we are trying to do," he explained to me.

"You mean, larger than this one?"

"Oh, much, *much* larger. Ours is actually quite small," he said.

"Really?" I responded in disbelief. "So where did you build this?"

We walked toward the main entry of QREC's building. On the left side was an opening. What looked like a small loading dock had been converted into a makeshift shop floor. A maker's garage. Hand tools like small power saws and impact drivers were scattered on the floor and tables. Come to think of it, I had noticed some people working there during the nights, wondering what they were up to. Now I knew. With no access to a makerspace, the students—all of them freshmen—had created their own.

The wind tunnel machine in front of the loading dock of QREC's building

Watching Joshua and his team gently reminded me of what I had been putting off: writing an e-mail to Hatch. I returned to my office. "We have some serious makers among our students," I typed. "This afternoon, a team of eight freshmen tested a wind tunnel contraption, handmade from wood panels, fans, and Arduino boards…I watched them for two hours as they conducted their experiment, and they were obviously very proud of what they had built."

I attached a photo of the machine to the e-mail. Even though I was just a bystander, *I* felt proud of what they had built. Joshua and his teammates were literally teenagers. Yet what they were trying to accomplish was radical. Truly innovative and inspiring, their enthusiasm contagious.

In his last year of high school, Joshua had tossed around his idea to several scientists. They unanimously declared with confidence that the idea was impossible.

In conventional methods, multiple generators were required to produce a tunnel with enough wind blowing from all different directions. The minimum at that point was to combine three. Each would be about two-thirds the size of the ones the students had built.

A huge amount of space and materials were needed, bumping up manufacturing costs to over 10 million dollars.[33] The sheer weight of the materials would add up to fifty to sixty tons. "Only NASA would have the budget to prototype something like that," said Joshua. He had just 500,000 yen (5,000 dollars) to spend.

He came up with an ingenious solution. Instead of blowing wind from multiple directions at the turbine from the *outside*, what if the turbine could be placed *inside*, with the

---

33   Joshua Lawn, "風光変動を再現できる新型回転風洞の開発 (Development of A Novel Rotating Wind Tunnel for Reproducing Fluctuations in Wind Direction)," in *Challenge and Creation (C&C) Project 2013 Report* (Robert T. Huang Entrepreneurship Center of Kyushu University, 2014).

testing machine revolving around it to generate the necessary wind? This would reduce the size factor.

As for weight, he was reasonably confident he could use wood instead of metal. He was inspired by the inventors who tried to build wooden airplanes. His father, who was an architect, had drilled into him ever since he was young how sturdy wooden structures can be by employing the right joining methods. He thought he could ultimately get the weight down to five hundred kilograms.

Joshua knew controlled experiments would be key. Through the projects he did in high school, he learned about the futility of trying to generate insights from statistical models using data collected from turbines in a natural environment. This led to a second, more technical issue that had been called out by the experts. Wind must circulate evenly inside the chamber, even while the machine is spinning. Controlling the turbulence would be a nightmare. His idea was to cancel out the fluctuation effects by strategically positioning special valves in the air inlets.

Driven by his dogged belief that he could succeed, he then devised a strategy that would enable him to execute. He applied to the 21st Century Program at Kyushu University. The program is unique in that students have the freedom to specialize in any field, provided they could convince a professor to be their supervisor by their junior year. He knew he needed training in both mechanical engineering and aeronautics. The engineering department's conventional curriculum was too constraining. He would rather cherry-pick the courses he needed to realize his dream machine. Therefore, he chose the 21st Century Program.

One of the first things he did after he was admitted in April 2013 was to systematically persuade every male student in his class to join his project. Unlike the engineering departments, the gender balance in his program was tipped overwhelmingly toward women. There was only a handful of men, and soon he had every one of them on board.

They also needed space. Once their project was funded through C&C, Joshua somehow convinced my colleagues at QREC to let his team use the "storage space" in our building for free. The team would have to commute back and forth between the new campus at Ito, which was where courses for incoming freshmen were offered, and Hakozaki. That meant more than an hour each way by train and bus.

The arrangement turned out to be perfect. In fact, in hindsight, had they set up shop at Ito, it is likely that they may have been shut down. The buildings at Hakozaki were slated to be demolished, and so oversight there was laxer.

A well-known management practice for nurturing successful in-corporate ventures is to keep the innovation-driven labs separated from the established organizational structure, essentially running it as a separate business.[34] For example, Jeff Bezos deliberately set up Lab126—the secret research and development (R&D) team that worked on the Kindle—in Cupertino, closer to Apple than to Amazon's headquarters in Seattle.[35]

Such projects are known as "skunk works," which is slang for "an often secret experimental laboratory or facility for producing innovative products, as in the computer or

---

34   Peter F. Drucker, *Innovation and Entrepreneurship: Practice and Principles* (New York: Harper & Row, 1985), Kindle.

35   Adrian Slywotzky, "The Real Secret of Kindle's Success," *Fast Company*, September 26, 2011.

aerospace field."[36] According to *The Economist*, skunk works "are modeled on the Lockheed aircraft company's secret research-cum-production facility where, in the 1940s, staff were removed from the corporate bureaucracy and encouraged to ignore standard procedures in the hope that they would come up, in the first instance, with a high-speed fighter plane that could compete with those produced in Germany by Messerschmitt." [37]

QREC extended to the students a level of freedom that was unusual within the conservative, paternalistic culture of Japanese universities. For all C&C student teams, the seminar rooms in the QREC building were accessible twenty-four seven; we trusted the students to be responsible. I learned later how impossible it is to provide around-the-clock access to space on campus. I have yet to win a single battle against administrators, who are adamantly against the use of project rooms after ten or eleven at night, usually for safety and security reasons.

There was no way Joshua's team could have completed the first prototype within the designated project time without the all-nighters they pulled at their makeshift garage.

They were able to collect reams of data during their experiment that February. Subsequent analysis showed that the revolving design really worked. A bunch of teenage freshmen had proved the professional scientists wrong.

The project was so successful, QREC continued funding it for the next three years.

Joshua became the first-ever student in Kyushu University's history to file for a patent through the university. He

---

36   *Dictionary.com, s.v.* "skunk works," accessed September 7, 2020.

37   "Skunkworks," *The Economist*, August 25, 2008.

presented his findings at an academic conference. His team won Best Technology Award at an international green tech competition in Taiwan.

The final couple of years became somewhat of a challenge. Demolition of the QREC building would begin earlier than planned, so they had to move their machine to another campus.

Their first garage was heaven compared to the other spaces they would come to occupy. The words "safety" and "sanitation" became part of their everyday lexicon. "If we left an extension cable lying around, we'd immediately get slapped with a warning," said Joshua.

It was also very important for students to have overnight access to fabrication equipment. In his spare time, Joshua liked to craft replicas of weapons, armor, and other gear from Japanese manga. He had a lathe, a CNC milling machine, and a 3-D printer in his apartment. He even welded on his balcony, accidentally charring the surface. "Luckily, no one noticed when I moved out," he confided to me in our interview. Joshua would sometimes sleep with the machines still operating. "If I notice a change in the sound, I would get up and immediately check the settings, and maybe add some oil."

QREC currently runs a makerspace available to its students. It is open until ten o'clock. "This is a real problem for students. Even though the machines can be kept running overnight, they come back in the morning to a bird's nest," explained Joshua, referring to the plastic mess a 3-D printer makes when it goes amok.

Enterprising students like Joshua are resourceful bootstrappers. They think and act like entrepreneurs and eventually find a way to breathe life into their ideas. Yet I shudder at the thought of an alternative outcome. What if there were no independent center to fund his project for four years in a row? What if the QREC faculty was unwilling to give them the space to build? What if they had been suspended for working on campus through the night? What if Joshua could not take all the high-level courses he needed to get the science and technology side of his project to work?

Ever since we first met, Joshua was clear and consistent about what he wanted to be: a scientist in academia. However, right before graduation, he took a fork. An alum who established a venture capital fund for university-related startups, Tsuyoshi Sakamoto, was so impressed that he talked him into founding a company to commercialize his idea. Sakamoto said to him, "You can always go back to school." Joshua was young. Even if he failed, he could always start over.

It was the right choice. "I look at the scientists we've hired, and they are so much more talented than me," he said. In his original application to Kyushu University, he wrote that he wanted to do research that had market potential. "80 percent of the researchers in my field are developing products nobody wants," he said. "They *totally* ignore the market."

His company, Japan Wind Tunnel Manufacturing Inc., has been expanding its product line and its employee base. They currently measure the performance of bicycles in addition to wind turbines. He has given up his hobby of producing manga memorabilia for now. "Monozukuri" or "making things" is a full-time job for him. He would rather do other things in his spare time.

Students have an edge over veteran scientists for one big reason: they are not overly committed to a particular technology or research agenda. Prior investments of time, money, and other resources can be a significant barrier when exploring new ground. These are known as "sunk costs" in business, and they are hard to ignore.

Students have the luxury of starting from the issues, not the science. They are also in the best position to tinker with new tools and platforms, sometimes for frivolous reasons. This was the case for Mark Zuckerberg when he developed FaceMash using the distributed servers at Harvard for comparing girls.[38]

One of the best ways to start a technology venture was for faculty to give their students a half-baked idea "and let them run with it," said Perry Samson, a professor at the University of Michigan. Researchers often have promising ideas they don't have the time, money, or inclination to follow up. A doctoral student took Samson's half-baked idea for an Internet-based weather service and created Weather Underground in 1995. The company was acquired by The Weather Channel in 2012.

I was seeing more and more examples of student innovations at makerspaces. Joshua was only the tip of the iceberg. "Three makes a trend," we used to joke when I was a newspaper reporter. If we found three examples, then we could write it up as an article. And there were significantly more than three.

But I also knew that makerspaces are expensive to build and maintain. I therefore pinned my hopes on a new opportunity. Hatch privately disclosed to me that a Japanese company was negotiating with TechShop to open one in Japan. I had fallen in love with TechShop and was looking forward to move my relationship to the next stage. Not all romances have happy endings, though, as I was about to find out.

---

38   Ben Mezrich, *The Accidental Billionaires: The Founding of Facebook, a Tale of Sex, Money, Genius and Betrayal* (New York: Anchor Books, 2010).

CHAPTER 3

THE RISE AND FALL OF COMMERCIAL MAKERSPACES

The first TechShop opened its doors in 2006 in Menlo Park, California, near Stanford University. Dan Woods, co-founder of *Make* magazine, recalled how it was "a scrappy space filled with used equipment and wildly creative makers."[39] By the time of my visit, the commercial makerspace chain was expanding rapidly, with ten locations around the US in 2017.[40]

"TechShop arms the do-it-yourself movement with up to seventeen thousand square feet of space and one million dollars of machinery per store to help individuals 'build their dreams'."[41] It partnered with companies like Ford, which

---

39   Dan Woods, "TechShop Closes Doors, Files Bankruptcy," *Makezine*, November 15, 2017.

40   Woods, "TechShop Closes Doors."

41   Karin Chen, *TechShop: A Case Study in Work Environment Design* (Deloitte University Press, 2013), 1.

gave out free TechShop memberships to employees who participated in an incentive program for submitting inventions. As a consequence, innovation submissions at the company increased by over 30 percent.[42]

Arizona State University was the first to open a TechShop on campus in November 2013. I was deeply envious. The makerspace was open to the public so students could benefit from the experiences of a larger community of creators. "They'll get to rub elbows with the entrepreneurs they want to emulate," said TechShop CEO Mark Hatch.[43]

I longed to connect with TechShop at a deeper level, and after years of waiting, the chance arrived. The first franchise in Japan opened its doors in Tokyo in 2016. It would be run as an in-house venture by the electronics company, Fujitsu. The timing could not have been better. I had just moved back to Tokyo to join the faculty of the School of Management at Tokyo University of Science (TUS).

The startup scene was heating up in Tokyo. TUS wanted to increase its presence and influence in creating innovation-driven enterprises. A year before I arrived, it had invested in MIT's Regional Entrepreneurship Acceleration Program, or MIT-REAP. As luck would have it, the president of Fujitsu was an alumnus. The company decided to join the program as a strategic corporate partner.

I soon learned that an executive of TechShop, Junichi Shimada, a Fujitsu engineer, also graduated from our university. One thing led to another, and by the following year, I was teaching courses where our students were using the digital

---

42   Chen, *TechShop: A Case Study*, 3.

43   Weldon B. Johnson, "Chandler Techshop Aims to Bring Ideas to Life," *The Republic*, November 15, 2013.

fabrication tools at the makerspace to produce prototypes and products.

TechShop Tokyo was located in one of the most expensive office areas in the city. It was on the second floor of the ARK Mori Building, just minutes away from the American Embassy and the Roppongi district. The building is something of an icon. It was Japan's first large-scale private redevelopment project, integrating office and residential housing with retail, a hotel, and a concert hall.

The makerspace was huge by Japanese standards: twelve hundred square meters with ceilings eight meters high. Fifty different types of machines enabled its members to 3-D print, laser cut, UV print, weld, lathe, woodwork, digitally dye, sew, and more. The eyes of students would always light up on the first visit. They also loved the free popcorn and coffee.

From the outside, TechShop looked mysterious, even dangerous. Concert-goers walking from Suntory Hall to the subway at night would sometimes eye the makerspace with mounting suspicion. "They thought they were seeing a Tepodon missile," said Shimada. Indeed, I could see how the tall, stainless steel canister used for steaming textiles might be mistaken for a North Korean missile.

Using the space came with a hefty price, however. Users had to take a class called a Safety Basics Unit, or SBU, for nearly every type of machine. They ran upwards of four hours, and cost over four thousand yen per unit. We could afford to pay for them for our students through a government education grant. I, too, needed to be able to handle the machines we would be using for class. So, I tapped into my research funds to take as many SBUs as I could squeeze into my hectic schedule.

You also needed a membership. Monthly fees started at 18,500 yen, about 50 percent more than the going rate for a gym. Imagine having to pay extra to learn how to safely use a treadmill, weight machines, or an elliptical. That would undoubtedly be a deal-breaker. Working out one's creative muscles turns out to be *very* expensive. Students could not afford to join, despite steep discounts.

Fees add up for two main reasons. First, large investments are needed to buy and maintain the machines. 3-D printers are dramatically cheaper than before, but most digital fabrication tools are not affordable for individuals. One of the most heavily utilized machines—laser cutters—go for thirty thousand dollars each. There are four of them on the shop floor. Plus, the more they're used, the more maintenance is required.

Second, overhead costs are high. Specialized staff need to be retained around the clock. Cost of utilities, especially electricity, run higher than a normal office. Although the building gave them preferential pricing, rent was still a significant burden.

Inevitably, tragedy struck. "We regret that TechShop Tokyo ceased operations on Feb 29, 2020."[44] After four years of trying, Fujitsu pulled the plug.

The writing had been on the wall. TechShop in the United States abruptly shut down all of its domestic locations in November 2017. The rapid expansion had taken its toll. Hatch left the company in 2016 and was replaced by Dan Woods, who had previously been COO.[45] Woods tried to pivot to a

---

44 TechShop Tokyo website, accessed September 7, 2020.

45 TechShop, "TechShop CEO Mark Hatch Resigning Position to Pursue Other Opportunities," *Global Newswire*, July 18, 2016.

licensing and managed services model rather than owning the locations outright.[46] The company continued to bleed cash. It delayed payments to instructors and vendors. Efforts were made to file for Chapter 11 restructuring, but in the end, funds were depleted and the company went directly into bankruptcy.[47]

TechShop Japan ended up with similar challenges. Their corporate parent could no longer afford to keep the startup alive, so the decision was made to close.

On February 29, 2020, I flew in from Hiroshima to attend one last workshop and the closing ceremony. I had changed jobs once again, this time to work for a university in more rural settings. I was commuting to Tokyo on a weekly basis to teach and supervise TUS students, including the TechShop course.

At that moment, COVID-19 was silently spreading across Tokyo. A woman in her twenties working at a hospital had been diagnosed with the virus, the thirty-seventh confirmed case in the city.[48] "Social distancing" was not part of our working vocabularies yet. Nevertheless, the closing ceremony was scaled down to a "small gathering" for members who wanted to be there for the last day. Everyone who attended was asked to wear masks. I brought my own white, oversized

---

46   Kenneth Wong, "The End of TechShop: A Huge Loss to the Makers and DIY Community," *Digital Engineering 247*, November 21, 2017.

47   Woods, "TechShop Closes Doors."

48   "新型コロナウイルスに関連した患者の発生について（第52報）(Number of Patients Related to the New Corona Virus (Bulletin No. 52))," on Tokyo Metropolitan Government's website, March 1, 2020, accessed September 7, 2020.

MUJI mask that I had originally bought to keep my lips from chapping during long, intercontinental flights.

I took them off briefly to sip beer from a bottle of Heineken. With the official speeches and words of thanks and applause over, I wandered toward Shoichi Arisaka, Managing Director of TechShop.

"I am so sad that I won't be able to finish what we started here," I said to him.

"I feel the same way," he answered.

We chatted for about ten minutes about how unfortunate it was that Fujitsu could no longer afford the operating losses. But we also acknowledged that maybe it was impossible for a commercial entity to maintain and operate a makerspace equipped with high-end machines in one of the most expensive and commercial rental space markets in the country.

I expressed my appreciation for all I gained through my four years collaborating with Arisaka's team. I was able to experiment with various course designs that could take advantage of the makerspace, some more successful than others.

In the last iteration, students designed campus novelty items that they had to make and try to sell. By then, I had a good feel for what worked and what didn't. I had ideas for bringing people from Hiroshima to TechShop to spark some new initiatives, and it pained me that this was no longer an option.

I asked Arisaka what he planned to do next. "The community aspect of TechShop is something that I want to bring forward into the future," he said. The space was special, but so were its people. "Maybe we can figure out something that my university can get involved with." I promised to stay in touch.

It was past seven in the evening and I was ready to leave. There was one last goodbye though. Ryota Yokoiwa was always easy to spot. I looked around the shop floor, where dozens of members were in the homestretch to finish whatever they were working on before the makerspace closed down at eleven. Yokoiwa was on the small side, but his blond-dyed hair and "STAFF" jacket made him pretty conspicuous. He was one of the longest employees there, and he had always gone out of his way to help me in times of distress.

I finally spotted him at the entrance. He was getting ready to take off the decal from the walls and doors. "The building owners are pressuring us to strip everything from the display windows and also clear the entrance. We're going to be spending the night taking everything off," he said. A tinge of sadness passed through me.

Yokoiwa had the demeanor of a soft-spoken artist. I later learned that he trained as an engineer and has a master's degree from the Kyoto Institute of Technology. He had been extremely knowledgeable about the technology behind the machines. I had no formal design or engineering education and would often find myself overwhelmed when trying to get something to work. He was very approachable, and I sought him out among all the other staff.

My desperate calls for help would often extend into longer conversations about the latest and cheapest equipment and what they could be used for. He sometimes showed me some of the products that he had designed and crafted on the floor in his spare time. One of them was a case designed specifically for holding the orange-colored box of CalorieMate, a popular Japanese nutrition bar. He sold it on Amazon and Minne, an Etsy-like site.

Priced at 1,200 yen, the case "is made from an FDM 3-D printer with very little post-processing. So, it is not the same quality as a commercial plastic product" according to the

Amazon listing.[49] It continued: "I have been personally having fun using it every day, so even if it is not exactly perfect, I would buy it. I figured there would be about one hundred people in Japan who might buy this, so I decided to put it on the market." Three customers liked the product enough to give it a five-star review: "Saw this on Instagram, and bought it through Amazon. The fact that a CalorieMate bar converts into a key holder is way more kawaii (cute) than I imagined. I love the roughness that comes from 3-D printing."[50]

Yokoiwa's 3-D printed energy bar holder

Yokoiwa was not sure what he would be doing afterward. We exchanged business cards, and once again, I promised I would keep in contact.

---

49 "カロリーメイトホルダー（ホワイト）(CalorieMate Holder (White))," Amazon, accessed September 7, 2020.

50 Ryota Yokoiwa, "カロリーメイト専用ホルダーをamazonで販売しています (CalorieMate Holder Available on Amazon)," *1101001000*, accessed September 7, 2020.

A week after TechShop closed, Yokoiwa sent me the following e-mail, a thoughtful reflection of his experience with makerspaces.

Dear Makino-sensei,

Thank you for coming on our last day. Pretty tired from all the cleaning up we've been doing every day. I knew that TechShop would close someday. And when it did, it would be tremendously tough because of all the stuff here. I never expected I would be the one doing the work.

He went on to share his initial encounter with makerspaces.

I think I first heard about the concept of digital fabrication around 2012. Around that time, I was invited to an alumni association meeting because they wanted to "hear the opinions from younger people" and I proposed they should make something like a fab lab on campus. I don't know whether that had any influence, but in about five years, a fab called the Kyoto Design Lab opened at my alma mater, Kyoto Institute of Technology.

A friend of mine worked there, so two years ago, I went to have a look. At the time, there was no dedicated building for the space, so equipment was scattered in various buildings on campus, but even so, apparently the facility was gaining traction as a hub that connected the siloed faculty and their students. I spent a long, long time as a student at this university, but it's so hard to believe that a digital fab did not exist on campus back then. Digital fabs and universities are really well-suited for one another. They enable students to expand the horizon of what they can achieve by a factor of twenty or more.

He then wrote about his transformation from engineer to designer.

> I myself graduated from engineering, but I specialized in theory. In terms of making tangible things using my own hands, I am practically an amateur. After some twists and turns, I am being paid for doing things like product design. This was only possible thanks to digital fabrication. This would have been unthinkable a generation ago.
>
> I was so happy to be able to talk to you on the last day.
>
> Hope to see you soon.
>
> Ryota Yokoiwa

I was moved. My romance with TechShop ended, but not in a bad way. "The essence of the TechShop vision was to develop a network of makerspaces, members, curriculum, standards, instructors, and learning that would fuel the birth of new technologies, products, jobs, and companies. TechShop has accomplished much of this vision," wrote Woods in a letter to the TechShop community in the US when it filed for Chapter 7 bankruptcy.[51]

Woods estimated that the spaces "led directly to the creation of thousands of new jobs; and helped generate billions in net worth and new technologies—some of them life-saving."[52] The tragedy was that they could never directly benefit financially from the innovations generated by its members. Accelerators like Y Combinator take an equity stake in the startups going through their programs. TechShop chose not to.

---

51   Woods, "TechShop Closes Doors."

52   Woods, "TechShop Closes Doors."

"TechShop was a grand experiment that touched the lives of hundreds of thousands of people," wrote the company's founder, Newton, in his closing message. "I'm very sad that we were not able to make TechShop into a sustainable business."[53]

As a commercial company, TechShop found it impossible to sustain its makerspaces without subsidies from foundations and governments. "This kind of funding is readily available to non-profits, and very rarely an option" for profit-making enterprises."[54]

For many years, the infrastructure for the original Internet was owned and operated by research institutions and universities using public funds, mostly from the Department of Defense.[55] It appeared that the time was ripe now for universities to step up its role in maximizing the value of makerspaces for delivering innovations.

---

53   Jim Newton, cited in Wong, "The End of TechShop."

54   Woods, "TechShop Closes Doors."

55   Leslie Berlin, *Troublemakers: Silicon Valley's Coming of Age* (New York: Simon & Schuster, 2017).

CHAPTER 4

THE SECRET OF EXPERT ENTREPRENEURS

There is nothing so practical as a good theory.

—KURT LEWIN

Saras Sarasvathy knew firsthand what it felt like to start a company. She ran a venture in India that manufactured plastic products using blow and injection molding. In the 1990s, she left her native country and crossed the Atlantic in order to study at Carnegie Mellon University (CMU) in Pittsburgh. She had a burning question. Picture a banker and an entrepreneur. They are probably very different. But how? Their taste in fashion? What keeps them up all night? Their hobbies? Their favorite drinks? Their motivations? Sarasvathy wanted to find out how they *thought* differently.

One of the courses she took was taught by the economist and cognitive psychologist Herbert Simon. He was a celebrity at CMU, having won the Nobel Prize in Economics in 1978. His entry in the *Encyclopaedia Britannica* describes him as a social scientist who "sought to replace the highly simplified classical approach to economic modeling—based on a concept of the single decision-making, profit-maximizing entrepreneur—with an approach that recognized multiple factors that contribute to decision-making."[56] In other words, he embraced the complexities of human nature.

One of the assignments for the course required students to conduct a scientific study using Simon's research protocols. Sarasvathy seized this as an opportunity to test her intuitions that bankers think differently from people like her. She recruited four of each to take part in her project. All of them had over five years of experience.

The study was a deep dive into how individuals perceived risk. Previous research at the time showed no difference between entrepreneurs and non-entrepreneurs in the *degree* to which they were willing to take risks. She devised some problems that could tease out thought patterns. She asked the research participants to think out loud how they would solve those problems. This "think-aloud" method enabled Sarasvathy to uncover subtle and surprising nuances in the inner logic the professionals used when they made a particular decision.

Each person took about an hour to go through five problem sets. One had them choose between two investment opportunities. Another was about introducing new products. Life-or-death scenarios were included to tap into their value systems.

---

56 *Encylopaedia Britannica Online*, s.v. "Herbert A. Simon: American Social Scientist," accessed September 13, 2020.

The results were then compared across individuals to explore common elements.[57] A simple cluster analysis of the data revealed two distinct groups, perfectly separating the entrepreneurs from the bankers.[58]

The details were fascinating. They showed that entrepreneurs attempt to control the *outcomes* of a situation. "Their approach was to pick an acceptable level of risk and then push for larger profits, selecting the project with the best worst-case scenario. They…expressed confidence that they could make the reality better than the worst-case probability."[59]

Bankers, in contrast, have a target outcome for which they try to control the *risks*. They also tried to avoid situations where higher levels of *personal* responsibility were at stake. In situations involving decisions on human life and health, "their suggestions were doubtful and evasive."[60]

In a trade-off between a cheaper option that reduced but did not eliminate workers' deaths, and one that could guarantee safety but was not affordable, the bankers all chose the first option because it "was better than doing nothing."[61] They did not suggest any creative ways for raising money to fund the expensive option.

------

57   D.K. Sarasvathy, Herbert A. Simon, and Lester Lave, "Perceiving and Managing Business Risks: Differences between Entrepreneurs and Bankers," *Journal of Economic Behavior & Organization* 33, no. 2 (1998).

58   Sarasvathy, Simon, and Lave, "Perceiving and Managing Business Risks: Differences between Entrepreneurs and Bankers," 212.

59   Stuart Read et al., *Effectual Entrepreneurship* (London and New York: Routledge/Taylor & Francis Group, 2017), 66.

60   Read et al., *Effectual Entrepreneurship*, 66.

61   Read et al., *Effectual Entrepreneurship*, 66.

Entrepreneurs, on the other hand, rejected the cheaper option outright. They actively considered how they could pay for the second option, for example, by "asking for volunteers, giving up equity, selling to a larger company, or cooperating with competitors to increase prices."[62] Feelings of control, responsibility, and personal values seemed to drive their decisions.[63]

Simon was impressed. Sarasvathy had gone far beyond what a typical MBA student did for a class assignment. So, when she asked him to supervise her as one of his last doctoral students, he agreed without hesitation.

This was in the midst the first Internet boom. People told Sarasvathy that a PhD in entrepreneurship "is an oxymoron—because it's like art that one cannot teach."[64] Nevertheless, she persisted. She was awarded a doctorate in Information Science and Entrepreneurship in 1998, according to her CV.

Right around this time, my mentor, Doris Drucker, was busy marketing her invention through a company she had founded. In one of our first meetings, Doris asked me what I wanted to study at the Drucker School. "Entrepreneurship," I answered.

"Did you know I am an entrepreneur? I started my own company for a device called Visivox."

"Visivox?"

---

62   Read et al., *Effectual Entrepreneurship*, 66.

63   Sarasvathy, Simon, and Lave, "Perceiving and Managing Business Risks," 208.

64   Rashmi Patil, "Like Science, Even Entrepreneurship Should Be Taught at the School Level: Darden Prof Saras D Sarasvathy," *Edex Live*, July 27, 2019.

"It was a device that lit up when a speaker was not speaking loud enough in a lecture hall. I used to sit in the back row of the audience when Peter was speaking, and when I couldn't hear him, I would shout out 'LOUDER.' So, I invented this device."

"When was this?"

"Many years ago."

It turned out that Doris had started her venture when she was eighty-two. She was interviewed by the *Los Angeles Times* four years later in 1997. "I have a lot of energy and play a lot of tennis, but it can get boring after a while," she told the reporter.[65]

Doris was approaching one hundred when we met. I was one of the two Doris Drucker Women in Leadership Fellows for my cohort at the Drucker School. She would take me out to lunch, usually to a Thai restaurant in a shopping center nearby. I have a small appetite, and US portions are huge, even for lunch, so I'd feel a bit embarrassed that I could never eat as much as her. "Eat, eat!" she would encourage me.

She no longer ran her business, but she still played tennis weekly and lifted weights. Doris would tell me many times, "If Peter had worked out like me, he would still be alive!" It is not as though he did not exercise at all. Peter liked to swim, and he would do so daily in their backyard swimming pool. His mind was as sharp as ever, and he continued to write until he passed away at age ninety-five in 2005.

"Did you ever ask Peter for his advice?"

"Yes, but he said he didn't know anything about venture businesses."

---

65   David Colker, "Doris Drucker Dies at 103; Memoirist and Wife of Peter Drucker," *Los Angeles Times*, October 4, 2014.

I was caught off guard. According to scholars, her husband's 1987 book *Innovation and Entrepreneurship* played a significant role in legitimizing the field of entrepreneurship in business schools.[66]

"Entrepreneurship is neither a science nor an art. It is a practice."[67] This single declaration had a profound impact because it changed how we thought about the topic. Startups were not founded by risk-loving people with a particular DNA through some kind of magic. It was something that could be *practiced*.

I bought Drucker's landmark book around 1998, when I reluctantly quit Nikkei America. Unable to type for long hours on deadline, I left journalism to work in new business development. I read and re-read the book until it was full of underlines and corners folded over. As much as I appreciated the philosophical insights, I was also frustrated. There was no method that could immediately be applied by novices like me (or Doris) to actually transform innovative ideas into businesses. Drucker's expertise drew on his experience consulting for established entities, not founders in rapidly growing startups.

In contrast, Sarasvathy's research and theorizing led to critical insights into the way expert entrepreneurs think and take action. Her theory of what makes entrepreneurs entrepreneurial called effectuation, is an instrumental framework and scaffold for effective teaching. It is so powerful that

66   Jerome Katz, "The Chronology and Intellectual Trajectory of American Entrepreneurship Education 1876-1999," *Journal of Business Venturing* 18 (2003).

67   Peter F. Drucker, *Innovation and Entrepreneurship: Practice and Principles* (New York: Harper & Row, 1985), loc. 74, Kindle.

Babson College, ranked number one in our field, took Saras-vathy's theoretical model and rebranded it as "Entrepreneur-ial Thought and Action (ET&A)"—a registered trademark.

Frameworks provide structure. They are like maps that can be used to navigate through a seemingly chaotic land-scape. Unfortunately, I had never heard of effectuation when I started teaching in 2013. So, after five years of studying management for my PhD, I still felt I was flying blind. I had no hands-on experience in venture business. I was, at best, an informed bystander, first as a journalist, and later as an interpreter.

After decades of unprecedented growth, Japan slid into recession and remained trapped in stagnation for over twenty years after the economic bubble burst in 1989. Meanwhile, the environment for enterprising individuals was downright hostile. People were shamed when they failed. Few people perceived opportunities to start new businesses, and early startup-related activities in Japan has relentlessly hovered at levels far below other developed economies.[68]

Even today, parents shudder at the thought of their chil-dren working for a startup. A friend of mine recalled how a mother of a new hire came to the Tokyo office of a ven-ture business and promptly burst into tears. She demanded explanations. She went on and on about how she could not understand why her son—a student of the University of Tokyo—chose to work at this strange and obscure place when he could have gone to a prestigious, blue-chip firm.

---

68   Mizuho Information and Research Institute, 平成３０年度創業・起業支援事業（起業家精神に関する調査）*(FY2018 Report on Entrepreneurial Spirit Survey)*, (Tokyo: METI, March 2019).

What makes entrepreneurs entrepreneurial? As a journalist, I assumed it was some kind of "spirit" because that was how we translated the word entrepreneurship into Japanese. In my heart, I knew this to be wrong. Postwar Japan was overflowing with enterprising businesspeople who launched what would become some of the world's most famous companies. They clearly did not lack entrepreneurial *spirit*.

The fog finally began to clear in my second year of teaching. I was observing an intensive summer course at Kyushu University about idea evaluation. Two colleagues from Chalmers Institute of Technology in Sweden, Karen Williams-Middleton and Mats Lundqvist, had been invited to demonstrate to our students how to assess technology-based ideas for commercialization.

Early on, Williams-Middleton introduced the core building blocks of effectuation. She talked about how the decision-making logic of experts can be useful for students. This was all completely new to me. "A framework!" I thought. Excited, I asked Williams-Middleton to guide me through some of the literature.

Our brains use a particular logic when we create something from nothing. It is different from how we think when we are managing or planning something that already exists. Kids are inherently entrepreneurial. They are not afraid to get their hands dirty. They are willing to go and try things out. If they can't figure it out on their own, they ask someone for help.

As we get older, we lose touch with the maker in us. Our thinking selves take over. We are conditioned to plan for everything, think through all the possible options, and settle on the one that is most likely to get us to the desired outcome. Business managers rarely question the validity of the

Plan-Do-Check-Act, or PDCA, cycle, which time and again has delivered results.

Except, it doesn't always. The research on expert entrepreneurs sheds light on why. Sarasvathy defined an expert as a founder with ten to fifteen years of experience running two or more businesses. Only two hundred forty-five people in the world qualified when she conducted her study.[69] Of these, forty-five agreed to participate.[70] Their companies had revenues between 200 million US dollars to 6.5 billion US dollars per year.[71] Based on my conversations with her, it was clear they were not the run-of-the-mill kind of entrepreneur. Some were probably iconic.

After analyzing over eighty hours of transcriptions, or more than five hundred pages of data, five principles emerged: bird-in-the-hand, pilot-in-the-plane, crazy quilt, lemonade, and affordable loss.[72] We will look at each one, but before we do so, it is useful to appreciate the context within which entrepreneurs operate.

The key is to be able to distinguish between three different states: prediction, risk, and uncertainty. If everything is completely controllable and known as in a laboratory experiment, it is possible to make predictions. In a more ambiguous yet relatively consistent environment like that of traditional finance, gathering lots of information and data can yield statistical models that minimize risks in decision-making.

---

69   Patil, "Like Science."

70   For the published study, the data of 27 participants were used.

71   Leigh Buchanan, "How Great Entrepreneurs Think," *Inc.*, February 1, 2011.

72   *What Is Effectuation?* on Effectuation.org website, (2011), accessed September 20, 2020.

An uncertain situation is one in which the future is totally unknowable, no matter how much information is gathered. Prediction is futile. Things hardly ever go according to plan because there are so many contingencies.[73]

The participants in the study were masters in dealing with the third state, uncertainty. They preferred using a fundamentally different logic from bankers and managers. Instead of using a causal logic to choose the best out of many possible means to get to a given end through execution, they look at their available means, imagine what outcomes they desire, then effectuate until they eventually ended up with something new.

To effectuate means "to cause or bring about (something): to put (something) into effect or operation" according to the *Merriam-Webster* dictionary. Action causes an effect. Thinking and meticulous planning doesn't. [74]

Causal logic is the antithesis of effectuation. It dominates most of society and how we think. The purpose of science is to identify causal relationships so we can harness the effects. Most corporate and military strategies assume causation. This mode can be counterproductive in situations ruled by uncertainty, such as in guerilla warfare during the Vietnam War, the current war on terrorism, the string of recent financial crises, climate change, and the COVID-19 outbreak.

---

73   Saras D. Sarasvathy, "Causation and Effectuation: Toward a Theoretical Shift from Economic Inevitability to Entrepreneurial Contingency," *Academy of Management Review* 26, no. 2 (2001).

74   *Merriam-Webster Online*, s.v. "effectuate (verb)," accessed September 13, 2020.

Japanese companies have had such a poor track record in delivering innovations in a knowledge-based economy because they have been applying a causal logic to uncertain situations. In contrast, makerspaces are an ideal place to deliberately practice a logic of creation, where students are encouraged to continuously act, learn, build, and reflect.

Sometimes old habits must be unlearned in order to acquire new ones. A quick and easy way to accomplish this is to push people outside their comfort zones. At a university, assignments and deadlines usually do the trick. A makerspace with structured programming where students are directed to work under severe time pressure and resource constraints is fertile ground for developing entrepreneurs and innovative new products and services at the same time.

Let us now go over the principles of effectuation. The first is to start with the means available to you rather than a given goal. It is called the bird-in-the-hand principle.

Second, set clear boundaries in terms of what you are willing to lose, whether it be in terms of money, time, or relationships. This is the principle of affordable loss. Students dread having to talk to real people to test their ideas until they are reminded that they actually don't have a lot to lose. They won't be fired. They can't lose money or reputation that they don't have. And they have already committed time to the program, which will eventually end anyway whether they succeed or not.

The founders of Airbnb had little to lose setting up a website and putting up a post seeking people who would want to sleep on air mattresses in their loft with breakfast, all for eighty dollars a night. They needed the extra cash to pay rent.

Three people showed up, indicating that their crazy idea may have traction.[75]

Third, failure is a matter of perspective. This is the lemonade principle, borrowing from the American colloquialism "when life gives you lemons, make lemonade." The unexpected is not a threat to be feared because the insights gained from failures can lead to a competitive edge.

For example, Airbnb failed multiple times before the business became viable. "The whole story around their origin takes a lot more twists and turns than most people who have read about the company know," says Leigh Gallagher, who wrote a book on the company.[76] The breakthrough came when Paul Graham of the Y Combinator accelerator program strongly encouraged the team to talk to their users, many of whom happened to be in New York City.

They quickly learned that the pictures on their site were a significant problem. They bought a camera and went door-to-door to improve the quality of the photos.[77] They helped users to "dress up their properties with better language, better pricing, and just gussied up the listings—and that was enough to turn the numbers to where they then started to catch fire."[78]

---

75   Rebecca Aydin, "How 3 Guys Turned Renting Air Mattresses in Their Apartment into a $31 Billion Company, Airbnb," *Business Insider*, September 20, 2019.

76   "The Inside Story Behind the Unlikely Rise of Airbnb," *Knowledge@ Wharton*, April 26, 2017.

77   Jasper, "The Airbnb Founder Story: From Selling Cereals to a $25B Company," *Get Paid for Your Pad*, August 8, 2019.

78   "The Inside Story."

Fourth, goals are tentative. They have to be because of the high levels of uncertainty. Focus on what you can control to shape and create the future. This is the pilot-in-the-plane principle. Sometimes, extraneous events may constrain one's means and goals. In extreme weather, a pilot may decide to divert the plane to another airport, thereby changing the initial goal. Improvisation, bootstrapping, and bricolage are ways through which expert entrepreneurs creatively generate new opportunities with limited resources. Airbnb would have died if their founders had not resorted to selling Obama O's and Cap'n McCain's cereal for forty US dollars a box, earning them thirty thousand US dollars. Their "bed" business wasn't working, so they focused on the "breakfast" side.[79]

Fifth, partnership is valued over competition. By continuously making "asks" to people who can help them, the means that are available expand. Bill Gates convinced IBM, a potential competitor, to be their partner *and* major customer.[80] One of Airbnb's first guests helped them with their presentations.[81] As more people and organizations commit to the venture, more means become available. Goals change accordingly, until eventually a new product, organization, and market emerge.[82]

---

79   Aydin, "How 3 Guys Turned Renting Air Mattresses in Their Apartment into a $31 Billion Company, Airbnb."

80   David B. Yoffie and Michael A. Cusumano, *Strategy Rules: Five Timeless Lessons from Bill Gates, Andy Grove, and Steve Jobs* (New York: HarperBusiness, 2015).

81   Aydin, "3 Guys."

82   Saras D. Sarasvathy, Effectuation: Elements of Entrepreneurial Expertise, New Horizons in Entrepreneurship, (Cheltenham; Northampton: Edward Elgar, 2008).

Universities are perfectly positioned for orchestrating partnerships. Commercial makerspaces and accelerators must invest in building up communities of practice. Universities are already embedded in an existing ecosystem that encompasses scientists, faculty, current students, and an alumni network that can be tapped for mentors.

Bill Aulet, author of *Disciplined Entrepreneurship*, says "the ability to build and be a productive member of vibrant and sustainable communities" is the most overlooked aspect of our educational efforts in entrepreneurship. It is important for students to be able to "creatively marshal resources they do not currently control, including knowledge, networks, and emotional support."[83]

Sarasvathy developed a dynamic systems model showing how these principles work together (Figure 1).[84] Her findings were published in the Academy of Management Review (AMR) in 2001.[85] It would take more than a decade before her work was available in Japanese.

---

83   USASBE, "Bill Aulet on "What I've Learned About Teaching Entrepreneurship"," *Medium.com*, April 8, 2019.

84   Sarasvathy, "Causation and Effectuation: Toward a Theoretical Shift from Economic Inevitability to Entrepreneurial Contingency."; Read et al., *Effectual Entrepreneurship*.

85   Sarasvathy, "Causation and Effectuation."

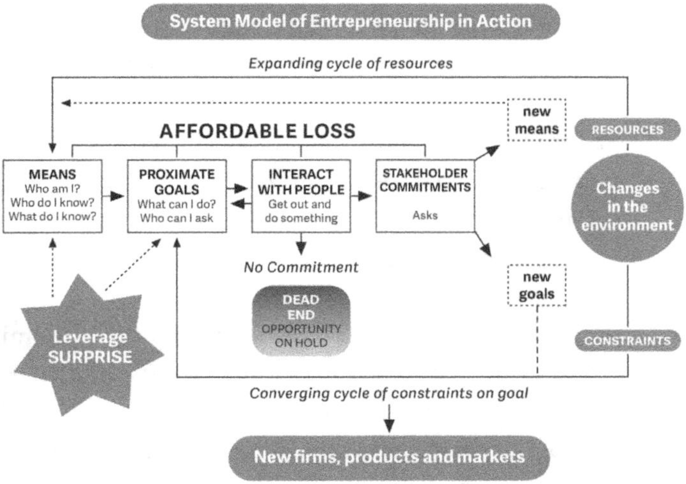

Figure 1 A systems model of entrepreneurship in action, created by the author based on Sarasvathy, 2001 and Read et al., 2017

In this model, campus makerspaces and the educational programs that are conducted there constitute the context and the environment in which students practice entrepreneurship. The provision of knowledge, information, mentors, project funding, access to equipment and so forth expand the students' available means. On the other hand, deadlines, screening processes and deliverables serve as constraints on the goals. The systems model can be useful for educators to diagnose and identify the challenges and opportunities for a particular student in developing entrepreneurial expertise.

After transferring to the Tokyo University of Science in 2016, I attended Babson's signature three-day program for educators. It was hands down the best training program I have ever taken. The four mantras they developed for students, which I refer to all the time in class, are a beautiful distillation of the core principles of effectuation.

- Start with what you have, not what you need.
- Don't be the best, be the only.
- Don't find yourself; create yourself.
- Action trumps everything!

Their trademarked ET&A framework was featured prominently, but there was never any mention of Sarasvathy's name.

I was initially shocked. Had Babson taken advantage of her? A couple of years later, when I invited her to come to Japan, I casually brought up the issue. No, she hadn't. "They asked my permission and I said, 'fine,'" she told me. In return, she asked only for the right to freely use the content they were branding. She saw value in spreading her ideas through Babson.

Not all academics fully support Sarasvathy's theorizing. One criticism is that the theory cannot be empirically tested because no stable system states exist.[86] Others point out that the influence of cultural and structural contexts is not fully considered.[87]

Chris Anderson predicted that the new industrial revolution would be well underway by now. However, we have yet

---

86 Richard J. Arend, Hessamoddin Sarooghi, and Andrew Burkemper, "Effectuation as Ineffectual? Applying the 3e Theory-Assessment Framework to a Proposed New Theory of Entrepreneurship," *Academy of Management Review* 40, no. 4 (2015).

87 John Kitching and Julia Rouse, "Contesting Effectuation Theory: Why It Does Not Explain New Venture Creation," *International Small Business Journal*, no. February (2020).

to see major disruptions or innovations of the likes of Google, Amazon, Netflix, or Uber that fundamentally changed our lives. The pandemic has only highlighted how much manufacturing *hasn't* changed.

In the chapters that follow, I will take you to a makerspace at the University of Tokyo that has quietly become a central hub for students developing cutting-edge technology-based products. Their stories demonstrate how effectual action, combined with digital fabrication technologies and structured programming, can accelerate the commercialization of science and bring us closer to the future Anderson foresaw.

PART II

GUIDING PRINCIPLES FOR CAMPUS MAKERSPACES TO FLOURISH

CHAPTER 5

HARNESSING PURPOSE

—

Masaki Takeuchi had never heard of laryngectomees when he began his master's degree at the University of Tokyo (Todai) in April 2019. During college, he attended a workshop for a proprietary voice technology intended for patients with the neurological disease Amyotrophic Lateral Sclerosis (ALS). While this would become the catalyst for his interest in developing solutions for people with voice disabilities, he was still searching for a more specific idea to pursue.

His co-workers at his part-time job at RIKEN, Japan's largest research institution, knew this. He had spent a gap year there, but was continuing to moonlight as a Todai student, at least until August. He was planning to apply to the Summer Founder's Program (SFP) at Hongo Tech Garage which he had heard about from other students at his university lab.

A few weeks before applications were due, his boss at RIKEN suggested he look into laryngectomees and a patient's association called Ginreikai. He ran a Google search and ended up watching YouTube videos.

He had heard about Tsunku, the famous Japanese music producer, who had lost his voice box to cancer. But watching footage of real patients was shocking and heart wrenching. "This is it!" He whipped up a proposal outlining his idea for a next-generation man-made larynx using artificial intelligence (AI).

When Katsufumi Matsui, director of SFP and the Garage, read his application, he immediately saw how complementary it was to another team's idea. Matchmaking was an important element of running the makerspace. He would make sure that these students would talk to one other on the first day of the program.

Masaki knew none of this, and he assumed that it was good old serendipity that he connected with his team-members-to-be during dinner on day one. "They were perfect," he said. The other two wanted to use their expertise in 3-D printing and audio technology but didn't know what for. Masaki had that something.

A hallmark of SFP is its intensity. Students hit the ground running, and they continue to sprint until demo day in eight weeks' time. The first challenge is perhaps the most nerve-wracking. Teams need a working prototype ready in a week, or they may be asked to drop out.

Deploy or Die. Borrowed from the motto of the MIT Media Lab under Joi Ito, students are expected to take this mantra seriously. The program is co-curricular, meaning it is not credit-bearing and therefore offered during summer and spring breaks. Students don't have to be there. It is entirely up to them to decide how much effort they want to put in.

SFP is clear on another point. The Garage will not teach students how to use the equipment on the shop floor. "We don't have the time," said Matsui.

Students who don't know how to work with digital fabrication tools essentially have two options. They can learn to use the machines themselves either on- or off-campus or find someone who can. This being Tokyo, TechShop was not the only commercial makerspace in town. There were at least three others, one being in Akihabara, the famous electronics district about fifteen minutes away by train from Todai's main campus in Hongo. FabLabs are another option, although there are only two in Tokyo.

Off-campus options in general are shrinking, as more and more makerspaces shut down like TechShop. The number of FabLabs in Japan declined for the first time ever in 2019. Smaller facilities and FabLabs operated by local municipalities have closed because utilization was lower than expected.[88]

Similar trends are seen globally. "Made in China: The Boom and Bust of Makerspaces" blared the headline of an article in Sixth Tone, a website covering news from China. "The government hoped makerspaces could help solve the country's innovation issue—but the push seems to have backfired." In Italy, only half of the registered FabLabs are still active.[89]

Students must take safety training in order to be qualified to use a particular machine at the Garage. Unlike the Safety Basic Units at TechShop, however, the Garage requires students to be self-sufficient from the get-go. The shop area is separated from the rest of the floor, and authorized users must tap their ID card when they enter and leave.

---

88   Gakuto Ochi, "【2019年版】日本のファブ施設調査—調査開始後、初の減少 2018年比15％減 ([2019] Japan's Fab Facilities Decline for the First Time since Survey Start: Down 15% vs 2018)," *Fabcross.com*, December 23, 2019.

89   Xue Yujie, "Made in China: The Boom and Bust of Makerspaces," *Sixth Tone*, November 8, 2018.

Garage staff wrote a simple, custom application that automatically sends a text message from the reader to a private Slack channel every time someone signs in. The channel can be monitored by staff like Matsui, even if they are not physically on-site. The text includes phone numbers, names of guardians (usually parents), and other important data that may be crucial in emergencies.

Engineering students typically learn to use 3-D printers and laser cutters as part of their course work. Masaki came to Todai for his graduate study because he was drawn to a curriculum emphasizing hands-on training.

But it was his first summer there and he needed to 3-D print right away. So, the only option left was the latter. Enrolling potential partners to come on board is an important element of effectuation. We over-glorify the entrepreneur as the lone hero who goes out to conquer the world. But in reality, most successful ventures have at least two founders, often with contrasting skill sets.

Apple Computer could not have launched without both Steves: Jobs and Wozniak. It is often said that the ideal team for a technology venture consists of three types: a hacker, a hustler, and a hipster. Wozniak was the hacker, the technical wiz, often an engineer. Jobs was the hipster, the designer who understands the needs and wants of the customer and delivers a product that people are willing to buy.

Apple was missing the third type, the businessperson, who has the hustling skills needed to create customers and markets. Jobs clearly had a purpose: making computers available to everyone in the world. Wozniak applied his engineering magic to convert Jobs' vision into a tangible product. Mike Markkula rounded out the team. A former marketing manager of Intel in his thirties, he was the linchpin for

Apple's success as a business, although he rarely came into the public spotlight.[90]

Steve Blank, founder of the Lean Launchpad classes at the University of Berkeley and Stanford, talks about how extremely rare it is "to find someone who can wear all the hats." This is the reason "why most startups are founded by a team, not just one person." In developing the initial classes, "We spent a year screwing it up…until we figured out it was about having the right team."[91]

Blank's programs for incubating technology ventures have been instrumental for the wide-spread adoption of the lean startup method in Silicon Valley and beyond.[92] Popularized by Eric Ries, it was developed based on Blank's concept of customer development in contrast with product development.[93]

Drucker proposed many years ago that the purpose of a business is to create a customer.[94] The lean startup method is a practical way to achieve this by eliminating uncertainty through the iteration of a three-step cycle: Build, Measure, Learn.[95]

---

90   Leslie Berlin, Troublemakers: *Silicon Valley's Coming of Age* (New York: Simon & Schuster, 2017).

91   Steve Blank, "The Startup Team," *Steve Blank* (blog), December 13, 2011.

92   Steve Lohr, "The Rise of the Fleet-Footed Startup," *The New York Times*, April 24, 2010.

93   Eric Ries, *The Lean Startup: How Today's Entrepreneurs Use Continuous Innovation to Create Radically Successful Businesses* (New York: Crown Business, 2011).

94   Peter F. Drucker and Joseph A. Maciariello, Management (New York: Collins, 2008);

95   Ries, *The Lean Startup*.

Blank decided early on that Lean LaunchPad applicants must apply in teams in order not to waste a week or more on team formation. As time went by, "we painfully relearned the lesson that team composition matters as much or more than the product idea. And that teams matter as much in entrepreneurial classes as they do in startups."[96]

He wrote in his blog post:

In a perfect world you build your vision and your customers would run to buy your first product exactly as you spec'd and built it. We now know that this "build it and they will come" is a prayer rather than a business strategy. In reality, a startup is a temporary organization designed to search for a repeatable and scalable business model. This means the brilliant idea you started with will change as you iterate and pivot your business model until you find product/market fit.[97]

Currently, SFP does not require students to have a team in place at the time of application. The University of Tokyo is at the center of one of the most vibrant entrepreneurial ecosystems in Japan. But even here, startup-related activity among students is relatively quiet compared to college campuses in the US. Students like Masaki, who are loners but have a sense of purpose and a solid idea, are encouraged to apply. This is essential for stimulating entrepreneurial activity so that a pipeline of student-initiated projects can build up.

That doesn't mean SFP will take everyone. Of the three types, they will generally *not* select hustlers who do not have either hacking or hipster-type skills. Most student ideas are

---

96   Blank, "The Startup Team."

97   Blank, "The Startup Team."

not refined enough to even begin considering business-related issues until much later. Matsui said that it is much more effective and efficient for them to look for mentors and advisors from their alumni network and match them to the students as they iterate.

The staff at the Garage go out of their way to increase the chances for good teams to form. In addition to proactive matchmaking, they try to design systems and processes that stimulate conversation. For example, students and staff all use Slack for program-related communication. Entry to the Garage is controlled by a digital smart key system.

Similar to the custom entry system to the shop floor, the main entrance is rigged to connect to a Slack channel that shows all comings and goings. The channel is visible to all active Garage users. That means you can always tell who is currently at the makerspace. If someone wanted to chat with Masaki and saw his name appear in the Slack channel, they might head over.

Eating together is recognized as an indispensable part of the SFP's programming. In Japan, university rules make it virtually impossible to cater food for students out of our operating budgets. The Garage and SFP is primarily funded through a corporate sponsor and is thus able to provide dinner every time the students formally meet. A refrigerator, microwave, and other cooking equipment are available for use. An alcove in the corner is slightly raised and lined with tatami mats for students to eat and relax. The students cannot spend the night, however, and must leave before midnight (or ten during COVID-19).

In one week, Masaki's team had a prototype ready. It was crude and scrappy: a small amp wired to a vibration device. But it worked. They contacted Ginreikai (literally, the "silver bells association" in English), which was founded more than sixty years ago to help laryngectomees retrain their speech abilities in order to "make a comeback to society."[98]

I remember quite vividly my own first encounter with a laryngectomee. I used to work part-time for Bilingual Group, a conference organizer and translation agency, and by sheer coincidence, Ginreikai just happened to be one of their clients. This was in the late '80s and I was in college studying international law. At some point, I was introduced to a Ginreikai member. While I don't remember the details, I was intimidated and felt uncomfortable talking to someone who had something embedded in their throat. Hearing their monotonal and robotic voice was quite jarring. Most of all, I remember my embarrassment, because in my mind I kept thinking I *shouldn't* be feeling scared.

Scientists had come and gone throughout Ginreikai's sixty-year history. Each time they came, its members would cooperate as research subjects with the hopes that a better device or method of speech would be brought to market, something that they could use within their limited lifetime. But science takes time. None of the previous research efforts ever resulted in any tangible improvement in the quality of life of laryngectomees.

Masaki believes that the Ginreikai members feel more invested in his team because of their purpose: to bring a product to market. "I think that's why they trust us so much," said Masaki. It probably helped that they were students, bursting with energy and enthusiasm and young enough to be their grandchildren.

"I don't want to let them down," said Masaki.

---

98   "Ginreikai Home," on Ginreikai's website, accessed September 28, 2020.

He set up their working prototype. One of the members volunteered to try it out. "Once we started, more and more people came over, wanting to test it too," he recalled.

Everyone was genuinely thrilled with what it could already do, and excited about its prospects.

Masaki Takeuchi tests the first prototype with a member of Ginreikai

The students kept refining their prototype and continued to visit Ginreikai on a regular basis. Then one day, Masaki began to sense a hint of dissent. One of the most important project goals was to help patients regain their original voice. "Eventually, they began to tell us what they *really* thought about our product concept," he said.

Masaki was shocked to discover that his core assumption turned out to be completely wrong. The biggest pain point for patients had nothing to do with losing their individuality, their ability to use their *own* voice. The trauma originated from the robotic, monotonous tone of reproduced speech. Regaining their personal voice was not a priority at all; speaking more naturally with modulations in somebody else's voice was totally acceptable. All they asked for was to sound more like a normal person.

This insight completely changed how Masaki's team defined the problem they were solving. Entrepreneurship educators live for these moments when students suddenly see what they couldn't before and discover that their ideas were flawed. Unique insights require hard work. No amount of searching on the Internet or reading market research reports will get them there.

I always tell all of my students that gathering information does not constitute action. Interaction is required with products, customers, or other resources, including money. Bill Aulet, who teaches entrepreneurship at MIT, regularly assigns his students a book called *Talking to Humans*, a practical guide for conducting customer interviews.[99] For many, getting out of the classroom to talk to strangers can be highly intimidating. Simply telling them so is ineffective, and many don't even try.

This is true of scientists too. In 2011, Blank was asked by the National Science Foundation to design a new curriculum specifically for scientists.[100] "Steve Blank Introduces Scientists to a New Variable: Customers" read the headline for a *Forbes* article about a government program in entrepreneurship called Innovation Corps, or I-Corps.

"From day one, researchers who arrive for class at Stanford University learn the most practical advice that every

---

99 Giff Constable, *Talking to Humans: Success Starts with Understanding Your Customers* (Giff Constable, 2014).

100 J.J. Colao, "Steve Blank Introduces Scientists to a New Variable: Customers," *Forbes*, August 1, 2012.

entrepreneur must master: Talk to potential customers. It's at the core of Blank's philosophy: The greatest product or service ever invented is worthless unless someone agrees to buy it. By the time teams return on day two, those who don't have feedback from ten customers are thrown out of the room."[101]

At SFP, physical prototyping is crucial for talking to customers. A prototype is the ultimate communication tool. Engineers may hate talking to humans but having something to show and tell can relieve a lot of the pressure. They don't even have to speak much. They could just point. More importantly, people give more specific and constructive feedback that, through iterations, can lead to a unique insight.

In a short program like SFP, time is the most limited resource. Speed is of the essence. Masaki's team was able to develop theirs because SFP made sure they could immediately go out and buy the materials they needed. The program gave them 200,000 yen (2,000 US dollars) for the project, which was deposited into Masaki's bank account before day one.

Navigating the arcane university accounting rules in Japan is like jumping into the rabbit hole in *Alice in Wonderland*. The C&C program which funded Joshua's wind tunnel project at Kyushu University requires students to follow all the strict (and sometimes excessive) rules for spending project money. Special authorizations, often taking weeks, are needed to disburse cash to students before their projects start. Reimbursements are also tricky. Credit card purchases need monthly statements in addition to an invoice and purchase

---

101 Colao, "New Variable."

receipts. This means students would have to wait as much as two months if they paid with plastic.

Such rules protect the university and taxpayers from fraud. Japanese universities, whether public or private, rely heavily on government funding, so financial accountability is a priority. But enforcing these rules are a significant administrative burden for running entrepreneurship programs. More importantly, they slow down projects and momentum, and can be detrimental to success.

SFP is financed through sponsorships, and as such, is not subject to all the accounting requirements that usually apply. Otherwise, Masaki would not have been able to deliver the initial prototype, or cycle through so many iterations so quickly.

Purpose, when appropriately harnessed, can be a powerful driver of innovation. It serves as a source of motivation to take action. It can also drive a willingness to learn and listen. A virtuous cycle where curiosity leads to commitment follows. Masaki says his commitment to commercializing a device grows stronger every time he meets with the people at Ginreikai.

Having a sense of purpose is one of three characteristics common to great innovators, according to Harvard's Tony Wagner. Wagner, an education scholar, interviewed leading innovators in the world about their childhood to see if there were common patterns in their education and upbringing.[102] The other two characteristics are play and passion, which we will look at in the next two chapters.

---

102 Tony Wagner and Robert A. Compton, *Creating Innovators: The Making of Young People Who Will Change the World* (New York: Scribner, 2012).

CHAPTER 6

PASSION AND PROGRESS

—

Mako Miyatake was like many other undergrads. She hated getting up in the mornings. The solution she created was far from typical. In fact, it originated from a movie. Literally.

In her junior year, majoring in computer science at the University of Tokyo, Mako was on the lookout for an internship. She had learned how to code in Ruby and PHP at her previous one. She Googled a combination of two words representing her current obsessions: robots and cooking.

"Connected Robotics was the only company that came up," she said. Among the many other companies she contacted for an internship, they were the first to respond. The reply came from the CEO himself the very next day.

She set up an appointment to meet with Tatsuya Sawanobori, who founded the startup that vowed to "innovate the kitchen by robots."[103] She took the Japan Railways

---

103   "Connected Robotics," on Connected Robotics website, accessed September 21, 2020.

train to Higashi-Koganei, a residential suburb in western Tokyo. Connected Robotics was headquartered at an incubation center at the Tokyo University of Agriculture and Technology.

"So, is there anything you want to make?"

"Well, maybe a breakfast robot," she answered.

"That's so cool! Would you like to give it a shot?"[104]

Mako loved watching movies, especially ones with a mechatronic feel, or "meka meka" as she described in Japanese. The *Transformer* series, *Mission Impossible*, and *Die Hard* to name a few. One in particular was the source of her idea.

In high school, getting up in the mornings used to be a breeze. She would rise to the aroma of a warm breakfast cooked by her mom. But no longer. She was on her own now. She fantasized about how wonderful it would be if a robot made toast, eggs, and coffee the instant she woke up, just like in the opening scene of *Back to the Future* starring Michael J. Fox.[105]

This was what she had in mind. Eggs, bacon, toast, and coffee prepared and served automatically. That same day, she was appointed leader and sole member of the newly created breakfast robot project at Connected Robotics. It was May 2018.

The startup has added dozens of employees in the two years since. But back then, it was just the CEO, her, and a

---

104 Ryo Ishii, "自動調理ロボットを作りたい理系女子！あの映画みたいに朝の時間を快適にしたい (A Woman in Stem Hopes to Make a Cooking Robot! Craving Mornings Like the One in the Movies) " *EMIRA*, June 26, 2018.

105 Robert Zemeckis, *Back to the Future*, (Universal Pictures, 1985).

few other people. Their office had two rooms. One was for engineering. She was assigned to the other one used mainly by the business side. She did her development there alongside Sawanobori, who was working on his own project, a takoyaki octopus ball robot. The engineers refused to let the CEO use their room because the smell of the popular Japanese street food was so overpowering.

As an intern, Mako did not have access to any fancy machines. She would use a fifteen hundred-dollar programmable robotic arm called Dobot Magician. It was designed for schools to teach children the basics of robotics. She didn't have any formal training in robotics, so getting the arm to open an oven door was as much as she could manage in her first month.[106]

Engineering was not a career Mako had envisioned. As a child, she had absolute clarity in what she would do when she grew up. She would practice medicine like her father. One day, she would succeed his clinic in Osaka.

Her parents assumed the same. Her goal was to get into Kyoto University, the most prestigious institution in western Japan. This was a matter of course. The private schools she attended had a disproportionate number of children whose parents were doctors. They all had similar aspirations to go to med school. Like her, they had been attending after-school "juku," or "cram schools," ever since starting in grade school.

Around the time she was sixteen, she had an epiphany. "I realized my reasons for wanting to become a doctor were vague," she admitted to the writer of the online magazine

---

106 Ishii, "自動調理ロボット."

EMIRA.[107] Her scores on the college practice tests said it all. "Oh my god. There's no way I'll pass," she thought. Mako could either aim for a lower-ranked medical school, or pivot.

She chose the latter. "I don't remember this, but apparently I suddenly declared in front of my entire family, I was going to be an engineer," she told me when I interviewed her at the Garage in late summer of 2020. "Fine," said her mother. "You should be an astronaut then." Space was not exactly in her plans, but she went along with it.

She was more into hackers and IT. In the movies, they were completely trusted to perform mission-critical roles, yet no one really knew what they were doing. Mako wanted to be able to understand what they did. Using logic and critical analysis, she boldly chose to target the University of Tokyo, or Todai, Japan's top university. "I figured that if I was going to go to engineering school, then it ought to be the one with the best facilities. Todai gets the most funding from the government," she reasoned.[108]

The clock was ticking, and the pressure mounted. No matter how much she studied, the best she could eke out was a "D" score on the practice exams. Todai was out of range.

November came around. Only two months left. With her motivation drying up, she looked up everything she could about the university in her spare time to get her into the right frame of mind. She even did what the Japanese call "image training."[109]

---

107 Ryo Ishii, "ソフトとハードを自在に！目指すは"欲しい"が作れるエンジニア (Moving Freely between Software and Hardware! Aspiration to Become an Engineer Who Can Build "Wants")," *EMIRA*, June 26, 2018.

108 Ishii, "ソフトとハード."

109 Ishii, "ソフトとハード."

Olympians use imagery to increase their chances of winning.[110] Dai Tamesue, a Japanese bronze medalist in hurdles, would simulate in his mind the day of a race in excruciating detail, from his mood when he woke up, how his feet felt when they touched the ground as he got out of bed, the color of the bus to the stadium, to the seat he would choose. If he couldn't see all of this, he couldn't win.[111]

Mako tried to visualize the details of college life by watching hours and hours of related videos online. One in particular struck a chord. It was footage from a Todai team competing in the NHK College Robot Contest, or RoboCon, in 2014. She was amazed by the ingenuity and engineering skills of the contestants. She vowed that this is what she would do if she made it.[112]

And she did. Mako immediately joined Todai's RoboTech club with about fifty incoming freshmen. She was one of only two women. She learned how to make parts from 3-D printers, milling machines, and laser cutters.[113] But robotics was not her area of expertise. She had only begun to dabble in programming through a coding program for women called Teatime Hackathon.

"In a sense, I was like a robot," she admitted, always taking orders from other people. She didn't feel like she was contributing. Although the club was "regimented in a good way," she felt ready to swap out the mandatory long

---

110   Christopher Clarey, "Olympians Use Imagery as Mental Training," *The New York Times*, February 22, 2014.

111   Dai Tamesue, Winning Alone (Tokyo: President, 2020).

112   Ishii, "ソフトとハード."

113   Ishii, "ソフトとハード."

pants and sneakers for skirts and more fashionable shoes. She dropped out.[114]

She continued making things though, mostly for her coursework. She played around with everyday items available at 100-yen stores like an acrylic iPhone case that she delicately shaved off by 0.7 millimeters to hold a smart card. She converted a lipstick holder into a USB stick.[115]

One of her quirkier inventions includes a motion-capture system for optimizing cotton candy-making. If you happen to be holding the candy-making stick too high, the app would signal "lower, lower." A photo of Mako holding a beautifully shaped cotton candy on a stick appears on her blog (though it's hard to tell whether this was the result of the app's advice, or if she is simply a cotton-candy master).[116]

A couple months before she started her breakfast robot, Mako walked through the doors of Hongo Tech Garage for the first time. She had a meeting there with some students. She found out that the Garage was hiring student staffers, so she offered to help. She also decided to apply to the Todai To Texas (TTT) program in July. Successful teams would fly to Austin in the following spring to pitch their projects at South by Southwest (SXSW). The annual festival brings together technologists, businesspeople, artists, and musicians for ten days to help "creative people achieve their goals."[117]

---

114 Ishii, "ソフトとハード."

115 Ishii, "ソフトとハード."

116 Mako Miyatake, "最適化わたあめ(Optimized Cotton Candy)," *Mako Miyatake Portfolio* (blog), October, 2018.

117 "About SXSW," on SXSW website, accessed September 22, 2020.

The university covered expenses for travel, accommodation, and exhibit fees. The program also provided marketing support. Since its launch in 2013, about fifty startups and project teams have gone to SXSW through TTT.

Mako was not even close to completing a working prototype. She didn't have the nerve to tell Sawanobori that she was applying to TTT. She decided to concentrate on two things that she had the ability to control: understanding potential customers and polishing her presentation.

Who would consider buying her product? Maybe hotels. A breakfast robot is both functional (it can cook) and entertaining. It could draw a crowd, similar to the eighteenth-century chess-playing mechanical Turk. Of course, there would be no one sitting inside pulling strings. Her robot would be the real deal.

She validated her hypothesis by talking to people about the idea and asking them questions. TTT chose her project, and less than a year from conception, Mako and her team went to SXSW to demonstrate "Loraine," the machine that cooked a full breakfast while you were sleeping. It was named after Lea Thompson's character Lorraine in *Back to the Future*.[118] A robotic arm turned the toaster and coffee maker on, and moved back and forth to place bacon, vegetables, and eggs onto a griddle.

Mako had recruited two other students to join her project, both from the RoboTech club. They used the Garage for project meetings and prototyping. They weren't working with a sophisticated one hundred thousand-dollar robotic system. That meant their design philosophy had to be different.

---

118 Zemeckis, *Back to the Future.*

Rather than improve the robot itself, they focused on how they could support and assist it. They 3-D printed custom parts for the robot's hand so that it could grab ingredients and handle other devices. They then designed specialized plates and shelves which they cut using laser cutters. This was to compensate for the arm's limited reach.

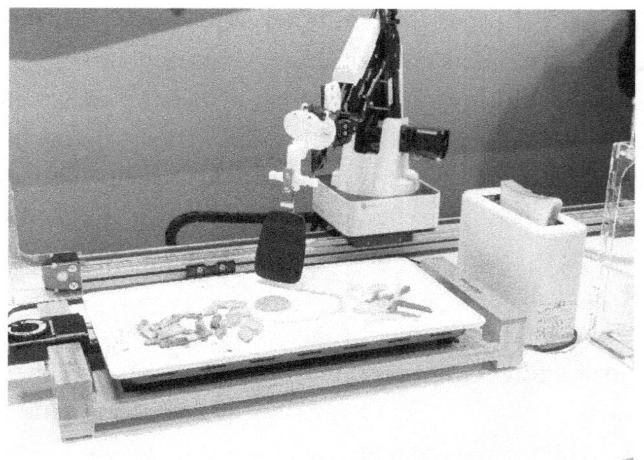

The breakfast machine in action

At one point, her team almost disintegrated. Mako was paying the price for her lack of management skills. She had no idea how to run effective meetings. She went to a student with more experience for help and learned about the value of facilitation and meeting minutes. Her team survived.

I first saw Mako on stage at the Smart Kitchen Summit in Tokyo, a conference attended by hundreds of industry movers and shakers from food to consumer electronics. She gave a short but powerful pitch about Loraine and her SXSW experience.

Mako Miyatake poses with Loraine at South by Southwest

We later stood side by side at the networking reception that followed. Students from Shinichi Ishikawa's molecular cooking lab at Miyagi University were giving tastings of frozen and carbonated ikura (the orange, bubbly cod roe, used for sushi). I wanted to try, as did Mako, whom I recognized from the pitch. We both sampled the frozen ikura, which literally fizzed on our tongues when the bubbles burst in our mouths.

I was not officially introduced to her until my first visit to the Garage in the fall of 2019 where, to my chagrin, I gave her advice she didn't really need. I casually said to her, "You should go and talk to as many customers as you can." Of course, she'd already done all that and then some. She was well on her way to practicing effectuation, reaching out to potential customers who may become her partners, while always testing key assumptions.

She was different from most of the students I encountered in the classroom in one crucial way: her passion.

Passion can be a double-edged sword. The entrepreneur's journey is sometimes called an emotional roller coaster. The startup process comes with surges of joy, troughs of sorrow, crashes of ineptitude, wiggles of false hope, and finally, the nirvana of the promised land, according to a graphic created by Patrick Collison, founder of Stripe.[119]

Student projects may not be quite as dramatic, given the limited time frame. Nevertheless, ups and downs are inevitable, and burnout is a real issue. My colleagues in Sweden at Chalmers University of Technology use an approach called appreciative inquiry to help students keep going in a non-destructive way, while also facilitating the identification of opportunities.

Appreciative inquiry is an organizational development method that focuses on strengths and what is working.[120] If I asked you to do an analysis of your company or organization, what would you analyze? When we did this exercise in class at the Drucker School, every single student looked at what was wrong with the organization. Just as we are conditioned to think in a causal way, we are also biased toward thinking of the world as problems to be solved. We rarely try to carefully consider what is working. "If it ain't broke, don't fix it," so the saying goes.

Appreciative inquiry was developed by David Cooperrider and his colleagues at Case Western Reserve University. It is known primarily as a consulting method in organizational

---

119   Andy Toth, "You Should Read This before Starting a Company," *Medium. com*, November 2, 2015.

120   David L. Cooperrider and Diana Kaplin Whitney, *Appreciative Inquiry: A Positive Revolution in Change* (San Francisco, CA: Berrett-Koehler, 2005).

development for change initiatives. More recently, some organizations are applying appreciative inquiry to drive innovation. My dissertation research topic was on how appreciative inquiry can facilitate organizational knowledge creation.[121]

In the context of entrepreneurship education, appreciative inquiry can be used as a coaching tool for students who find themselves stuck and/or overwhelmed. The method goes through four stages called the 4-D cycle: Discover, Dream, Design, Deploy.[122] The key to the discover stage is to analyze strengths and accomplishments. Asking students to reflect upon and share their peak experiences during the project can help them appreciate how much progress they have made.

According to research by Teresa Amabile and Steven Kramer, the best way to drive innovative work is for teams to recognize the small wins in their work. In their article for the *Harvard Business Review*, they wrote: "Through exhaustive analysis of diaries kept by knowledge workers, we discovered the *progress principle*: Of all the things that can boost emotions, motivation, and perceptions during a workday, the single most important is making progress in meaningful work. And the more frequently people experience that sense of progress, the more likely they are to be creatively productive in the long run."[123]

The remaining three Ds in appreciative inquiry are well aligned to the method of effectuation in conjunction with a

---

121   Emi Makino, "Appreciative Inquiry Summits and Organizational Knowledge Creation: A Social Systems Perspective" (PhD diss., Claremont Graduate University, 2013).

122   Cooperrider and Whitney, *Appreciative Inquiry.*

123   Teresa Amabile and Steven j. Kramer, "The Power of Small Wins," *Harvard Business Review*, May 2011.

campus makerspace. Students are encouraged to dream what is possible (imagining ends from means at hand), design the ideal future with the help of partners, and then deploy the design quickly through rapid prototyping.

What if a student is enthusiastic but not *passionate*? Are such students doomed to fail as entrepreneurs? Recent research tells us that entrepreneurial effort can actually stimulate what is defined as "an intense positive emotion, similar to excitement and elation."[124] For it to develop, though, there needs to be progress in the new venture. Self-intent moderated the relationship. If someone is pressured from the outside to do something, then passion is less likely to develop. Intrinsic motivation is therefore important.

On the day of our interview, Mako was about to submit an academic research paper featuring her project. She was one of the few students at the Garage, due to limitations from COVID-19. On a whiteboard, she had written dozens of words in English to see if she could find a catchy combination that might describe her new ideas. As usual, her enthusiasm was contagious, and I ended up spending at least ten minutes with her to explain the finer nuances of some of the words she had picked.

For years, scientists ignored the role of positive emotions and pretty much exclusively focused on the negative end of the spectrum, like mental illnesses, stress, and depression.

The science of positive psychology is still relatively new, with rigorous research emerging at the turn of this century. Barbara Fredrickson, a pioneer in this field, posited

---

124 Michael Gielnik et al., ""I Put in Effort, Therefore I Am Passionate": Investigating the Path from Effort to Passion in Entrepreneurship," *Academy of Management Journal* 58, no. 4 (2015).: 1013.

that positive emotions evolved so that we can broaden our horizons and build resources.[125] If her theorizing is correct, positive emotions are foundational for developing innovation and creating innovators. Since play is a common source of positive emotions, it is understandable why Tony Wagner identified it as the third element found in the upbringing of creative innovators. This is what we will look at in the next chapter.

---

125   Barbara L Fredrickson, "What Good Are Positive Emotions?" *Review of General Psychology* 2, no. 3 (1998).

CHAPTER 7

PLAY FOR PERFORMANCE

As a class assignment, I regularly ask students to create a "still life" photo that reflects who they are and what matters to them in life. They pick out five objects in their homes, plus one piece of nature (flowers, plants, etcetera), arrange them in a composition, and then take a photo with their phones. More often than not, students select something that represents what they like to play, like a tennis racket, a soccer ball, a game controller, or a musical instrument.

If Kazme Egawa were in my class, he would surely have chosen a surfboard. His undergrad days were spent playing American football and trying to ride waves. The latter turned out to be harder than he thought. Almost a year went by before he was able to merely stand up. Getting the timing right was really difficult.

Kazme had been practicing on his own. He learned much later that his persistence was actually unusual. "Most people give up on their first try," his surfing buddies told him. Learning the sport can be both lonely and bewildering. You don't have the luxury of an instructor by your side who teaches you like a swimming instructor can.[126]

Jane Chen, co-founder of Embrace Innovations, after a year and a half of surfing, said in a guest lecture at Stanford, "(I)t's so humbling, because most of the time I'm not on my board, I'm falling off my board, and having to find the courage to get back on, and paddle back out for the next wave." Chen continued, "And to me, this is the most important trait of being an entrepreneur, persistence and tenacity, because you will inevitably fail. Over and over again."[127]

Failure is not an option when you learn to play anything. It felt like such a shame to Kazme that others would give up surfing so soon. Was there anything he could do to help others learn better on their own? After nearly three years, the proverbial light bulb lit up in his head.

One of the problems Kazme faced as a novice was that he could not tell how the waves affected his board and his posture. The complexity can be overwhelming. So many physical variables are interacting that it's hard for beginners to know how to adjust their position in a meaningful way.

This was the problem Kazme wanted to solve when he showed up at Hongo Tech Garage in February 2017 for the Spring Founder's Program (SFP). By then, he was a master's student. His idea was to embed a surfboard with multiple sensors and LED lights. Accelerometers could sense whether it was going faster or slowing down. Angular velocity sensors could calculate which way it was heading. LED lights

---

126 Kotaro Muramatsu, "Todai to Texas ユニークな発想と技術で世界に挑戦," *Todai Shimbun Online*, March 20, 2019.

127 Jane Chen, "Embrace the Entrepreneurial Journey," *Entrepreneurial Thought Leaders* (Stanford eCorner, October 26 2016).

arranged on the edges could light up blue or red when accelerating or decelerating, and yellow or green when going right or left.

For the first prototype he showed at the Garage, he pasted a bunch of LED lights on a skateboard with some sensors. He didn't want to haul a surfboard on the train during rush hour. His lab in automotive production was at the Komaba campus, more than thirty minutes away from Hongo. So, with the two hundred thousand yen provided by SFP, he bought a surfboard he could mess with and a bunch of LEDs and sensors. He kept them at his apartment and worked on the prototype there.

"Does that mean that you didn't use the Garage at all?" I asked him.

"No, I *did* go quite often," he answered, a little defensively. All SFP students attend weekly meetings and lectures at the Garage during the program. Kazme added that he particularly liked it there because he could talk to other team members. He felt like he was with people like himself, "the crazy ones."

Kazme's observation was that surfing instructors would try to be helpful and say something like, "Please stand up when you feel pushed by the waves!" That kind of advice is not very logical, especially for beginners. So, he was going to develop a surfboard that would shine to signal the right timing.[128]

Once a decent prototype was done, he wanted somebody to test it. Kazme certainly did not have the skills. He decided to ask Kenta Ishikawa, the 2015 All Japan Surfing champion, who happened to be a neighbor of one of his surfing buddies

---

128　Muramatsu, "Todai to Texas."

in Shonan. Ishikawa was already quite familiar with his idea. After all, he had listened to Kazme talk for hours on end about the idea for lighting up a surfboard. Indeed, Ishikawa was the one who encouraged him to go ahead and just do it.[129]

Kazme wanted a pro to try the prototype to test whether it functioned. Although the target users were beginners, he had no idea what the surfing implications were with the additional sensors and lights. He also wanted feedback from an advanced surfer's point of view.

Ishikawa paddled into the waters of Shonan Beach. As Kazme watched Ishikawa deftly maneuver the prototype board on the water, his mind began to drift. He marveled at Ishikawa's performance on the waves. Ishikawa was in great shape. He was training for the 2020 Olympics, where surfing was making an Olympic debut. The prototype was working. The board would light up in blue or red or green or yellow, in synch with Ishikawa's moves. The colored lights were eye-catching.

Soon, Kazme noticed that Ishikawa was experimenting. He would purposely swerve to the left to make the board go green or decelerate to go red. Kazme's original idea was to have the board communicate to its user what it was doing. Ishikawa had turned the interaction around. The user would move to tell the board what to do. The result: a spectacle that was entertaining to watch from the shore. Exhibitions are a staple of professional sports like figure skating. The lighting could broaden the repertoire of expression, making it interesting and enjoyable for both the surfer and audience.

Kazme aspired to go to SXSW with his smart surfboard. He befriended a surfer at his internship at Rhizomatiks

---

129 Muramatsu, "Todai to Texas."

Research, then talked Masahide Chiba into joining his team. Masahide was highly skilled at 3-D modeling. While they sometimes butted heads about the project, they shared a love for surfing and a conviction that they could expand the possibilities of the sport.[130]

If they were to exhibit at SXSW, they had to make an impact. Visuals would be key. They decided to 3-D print a semi-transparent board. Strings of rainbow-colored lights would show through, resembling a jellyfish lighting up the ocean. This inspired them to christen their invention, jellyboard. The team applied for the Todai To Texas program, and was selected.

Entrepreneurship educators emphasize the importance of play for teaching students to be more enterprising and innovative. "The practice of play is about developing a free and imaginative mind, allowing one to see a wealth of possibilities, a world of opportunities, and a pathway to more innovative ways of being entrepreneurial."[131]

We tend to associate play with childhood, or leisure and recreation. It is recognized and protected as a basic right for children under the age of eighteen under the United Nations Convention on the Rights of the Child. "The right to relax and play (Article 31) and the right to freedom of expression (Article 13) have equal importance as the right to be safe from violence (Article 19) and the right to education (Article 28)."[132]

---

130   Muramatsu, "Todai to Texas."

131   Heidi M. Neck, Patricia G. Greene, and Candida G. Brush, *Teaching Entrepreneurship: A Practice-Based Approach* (Cheltenham; Northampton: Edward Elgar, 2014), 25.

132   UNICEF, "Convention on the Rights of the Child Text," accessed October 13, 2020.

Tony Wagner found that all of the creative innovators he interviewed grew up immersed in play, especially unstructured activities such as building things with Lego bricks. Their parents encouraged them, and through the learning and exploration that followed, the innovators-to-be satiated their curiosity. [133]

The framework for teaching entrepreneurship used at Babson College starts with play. It is followed by the practices of empathy, creation, and experimentation, with reflection at its center.

A defining characteristic of play is its nature of being "voluntary and superfluous, filling no basic need except enjoyment."[134] This does not fit the traditional image of a college classroom. The importance of active, experiential learning is well-accepted. In order to develop even more effective programs, we have to do better at creating "a playful, engaging, challenging, and enjoying experience" for our students. [135]

"Fun," according to Raph Koster, a legendary game designer, "is just another word for learning."[136] Fun stimulates the reward center of our brain that emits a neurochemical substance called dopamine, which encourages us to keep trying, even in the face of challenges and failure.[137]

---

133 Tony Wagner and Robert A. Compton, *Creating Innovators: The Making of Young People Who Will Change the World* (New York: Scribner, 2012).

134 Neck, Greene, and Brush, *Teaching Entrepreneurship*, 28 citing Huizinga, 1944.

135 Neck, Greene, and Brush, *Teaching Entrepreneurship*, 38.

136 Ryan Rigney, "A Game Design Legend Revisits His Theory of Fun," *Wired*, November 18, 2013.

137 Andrew Westbrook and Todd S. Braver, "Dopamine Does Double Duty in Motivating Cognitive Effort," *Neuron* 89, no. 4 (2016).

Research in psychology gives credence for why we should be infusing more play into higher education. Whether we are practicing for a game, an instrument, or a sport, we often get so engaged in the activity that we lose track of time and no longer feel any self-consciousness. This psychological state is called flow. In sports, it is sometimes known as getting in the "zone."[138]

People have experienced flow from ancient times. Mihaly Csikszentmihalyi, a prominent psychologist born in Hungary, gave the state a name. In his studies of the world's creative geniuses, his interviewees would talk about "being in the flow" when asked about their creative processes, and hence the naming.[139]

"You should come to the Drucker School because you'll have the opportunity to take classes with Mike," said Ira Jackson, the school's dean, referring to Csikszentmihalyi by his nickname. It was the fall of 2007 and I was thinking of applying to several business schools. I was attending a reception hosted by the school, telling Jackson that I was worried about choosing the school because Peter Drucker had passed away in 2005 and I would not be able to take classes with him.

I was a huge fan of Drucker's body of work since reading *Innovation and Entrepreneurship* in the late '90s. I thought I would die from envy when a few weeks after our second child was born in 2004, my husband, a journalist, spent three weeks in Claremont, California, interviewing Drucker for a month-long series of articles that would run in Japanese in *The Nikkei*. Postpartum blues were making me irrational,

---

138   Mihaly Csikszentmihalyi, Flow: The Psychology of *Optimal Experience* (New York: Harper & Row, 1990).

139   Csikszentmihalyi, *Flow*.

and I spent many nights feeling tormented by the fact that my husband got to spend time with Drucker while I was spending sleepless nights with a newborn.

"Mike is a *giant* in his field. Even President Clinton has read his book, *Flow*. You should take a look at it," said Jackson. I had never heard of him. I took a mental note of the book's title but did not bother to follow up.

A few weeks later, the school offered me a scholarship in Doris Drucker's name specifically for international women. I decided to accept. There was a slight complication, however: I was pregnant again. I was due to deliver in May, a few months before the MBA program started.

In my second trimester, I was suddenly admitted to the hospital. I was in danger of giving birth prematurely. I was immediately ordered to lie in bed for a week, keeping as still as possible. I was not allowed to go to the bathroom on my own, even though it was literally a few meters from my bed.

With nothing else to do, I looked for Csikszentmihalyi's book *Flow* on Amazon. I downloaded the book it onto a pocket-sized handheld device using a special reader. Despite the tiny screen, I devoured the book. Jackson was right. Taking courses with Csikszentmihalyi (pronounced "chick sent me high") would be priceless.

Flow is about the psychology of optimal experience when people "are so involved in an activity that nothing else seems to matter."[140] "(I)n the long run optimal experiences add up to a sense of mastery—or perhaps better, a sense of *participation* in determining the content of life—that comes as close to what is usually meant by happiness as anything else we

---

140 Csikszentmihalyi, *Flow*, 4.

can conceivably imagine."[141] Like play, the flow state is often associated with leisure, sports, and art.

When I reflected upon my own experiences as I read the book, I most often felt I was in flow while working as a simultaneous interpreter. When I am performing optimally, I am in deep concentration. But there is a paradox. I am extremely challenged, yet I am able to direct my attention to the task effortlessly. The experience is not quite the same as fun and enjoyment. Nevertheless, I am performing at my best, and I feel the urge to replicate the experience.

One of the things I learned in Csikszentmihalyi's class is that the structure of work is highly compatible with the conditions that enable the flow experience. There is "a clear set of goals that require appropriate responses." The activities "provide immediate feedback." In terms of a person's skills, they "are fully involved in overcoming a challenge that is just about manageable." Under these conditions, "attention becomes ordered and fully invested" and therefore we become completely focused.[142]

Csikszentmihalyi points out that when we are in flow, we are not necessarily happy. "The surgeon can't afford to feel happy during a demanding operation, or a musician while playing a challenging score. Only after the task is completed do we have the leisure to look back on what has happened, and then we are flooded with gratitude for the excellence of the experience—then in retrospect, we are happy."[143]

---

141   Csikszentmihalyi, *Flow*, 4.

142   Mihaly Csikszentmihalyi, *Finding Flow: The Psychology of Engagement with Everyday Life* (New York: BasicBooks, 1997), 28.

143   Csikszentmihalyi, *Finding Flow*, 32.

For the students at the Garage, their work is like play. During the SFP, students are under constant pressure to meet deadlines and show progress. It requires a huge commitment in time and energy, but they are there because they *want* to be there. They work hard, but it isn't *real* work.

Takaaki Umada, director of the Garage and founder of SFP, is adamant about referring to student activities as "side projects." The mission of university entrepreneurship programs should not be about creating startups. Students come for a very specific reason: to leave with an academic degree in the domain of their choosing.

When students come to Umada for advice on whether they should start a company while still in college, he is generally very cautious about encouraging them to do so. I cannot agree with him more. I cringe every time I see someone taunting students to become entrepreneurs right now and go all-in to launch their venture.

Play can be a useful first stepping-stone for students for producing passion and purpose. One student I met in the most recent batch of the SFP is developing a robot arm that can whisk authentic matcha green tea.

"I joined the Sado (tea ceremony) club at Todai when I came to college," explained the student. "It takes time and practice to prepare matcha green tea," he said. He is working on modifying a robot arm to hold a matcha tea whisk (chasen). He showed me the custom parts he made using a laser cutter and 3-D printer to attach the whisk to the arm.

So far, he had succeeded in getting the robot to whip up the green tea. He has yet to figure out how to automatically add the green tea powder and control the water temperature. It was clear that he found this endeavor fun. He wanted to develop a system that could be used in cafes so that more people can enjoy genuine matcha green tea, the unsweetened variety, unlike the syrupy latte versions often found in cafes.

He has subsequently moved on to another project. The flexibility and freedom to try new things when something is not working is an important aspect of practicing entrepreneurship.

Analogies might be drawn to practicing how to play a musical instrument. Beginners start with a simple song that is enjoyable, then move on to more difficult pieces. A typical progression seen at the Garage is for students to fail three times before getting to success. Initially, they try out an idea for something that they personally would want to buy. The next time, they start with a specific set of customers in mind. In the third iteration, they work toward solving a real problem. By then, they may have come to a unique insight that becomes the seed for a viable venture.

Experts are not born. They develop over time through deliberate practice. According to K. Anders Ericsson, who is best known for his study of experts, four conditions need to be met. Students must be given well-defined tasks. They have to be motivated to improve. Feedback is required. Finally, there should be ample opportunity for repetition and gradual refinements of their performance.[144]

Kazme intuited Ericsson's theory when he was learning how to surf. His idea was to provide beginners who were practicing on their own the missing element, which he thought was feedback. The jellyboard would be the feedback mechanism.

Student activities at the Garage are mostly unstructured. In reality, Matsui and Umada put in a lot of effort to have

---

144 K. Anders Ericsson, "Deliberate Practice and Acquisition of Expert Performance: A General Overview," *Academic Emergency Medicine* 15, no. 11 (2008).

scaffolds in place to facilitate learning. First, the program is bounded by time: two months. There is a fixed budget. Assignments with tangible deliverables must be completed.

The projects are formally critiqued twice during the eight weeks. Prominent investors and entrepreneurs from the startup community in Tokyo are invited to give feedback to students on their pitches; once midway through the program, and then for the final presentations. Most of them are alum, eager to mentor the next generation.

Friendly competition between the student teams in each batch gives an additional motivational push. At the end of the summer program, many of them submit to Todai To Texas for a chance to go to SXSW. In the spring, the best projects apply for competitive funding through the MITOU (pronounced "me-toe") program, which aims to "to discover and develop young talents called 'Creators' who are capable of accelerating innovation and playing a key role in creating next-generation IT markets."[145] The Garage also has a gap fund for those who want to continue working on their projects during the school year.

In addition to financial support, these awards and grants can provide external validation of their ideas. It is as though they are playing a game that has a certain set of rules and criteria for success, with the potential of winning real prize money and recognition. In the MITOU program, SFP students have been phenomenally successful in reaping financial benefits ranging from 3 million yen (30,000 US dollars) for individuals, and up to 10 million yen (100,000 US dollars) for projects.

---

145 "MITOU Program," on Information-technology Promotion Agency's website, accessed October 13, 2020.

Interestingly, Umada and Matsui have been very careful to stay quiet about the string of awards and research funding their students have won since the Garage's inception. It is tempting to count the number of startups founded, the amount of money raised, and the awards that have been won, so as to demonstrate the Garage's effectiveness in developing entrepreneurship. Not only is this counterproductive, but it is also downright harmful. It puts our eyes on the wrong ball.

Ultimately, our mission is to help students practice *how* to fish. Whether they catch small fry or a massive tuna or none at all doesn't really matter. In fact, *failing* to raise money for a project also serves an important purpose. Some students have a hard time deciding when to stop working on a project. In the practice of effectuation, if one is not able to get commitments from other stakeholders, the opportunity is put on hold. It is a dead end. Time to move on.

So, it doesn't matter if a project fails or succeeds. The more you experience flow while practicing, the more likely you are to perform optimally and achieve results. A sense of accomplishment encourages us to keep going, even in the face of the inevitable setbacks. A virtuous cycle of performance kicks in, raising not only the possibilities of real innovation to happen, but also, in the case of failure, the willingness to go and play again. As Wayne Gretzky said, "You miss 100 percent of the shots you don't take."

Kazme continues to swing away. When we spoke on Zoom, I asked him how he was able to continue practicing surfing on his own for such a long time. I had imagined him on the beach after hours of trying to catch waves, calling it a day, and then taking a train back to his apartment, all alone. This was not the case. He'd always visit his friend's house in Shonan, where he'd be treated to a family dinner.

The conversation would inevitably turn to surfing. Kazme would tell his friend's father, also a surfer, about his trials and tribulations of the day in the water. For Kazme, it was like a home away from home.

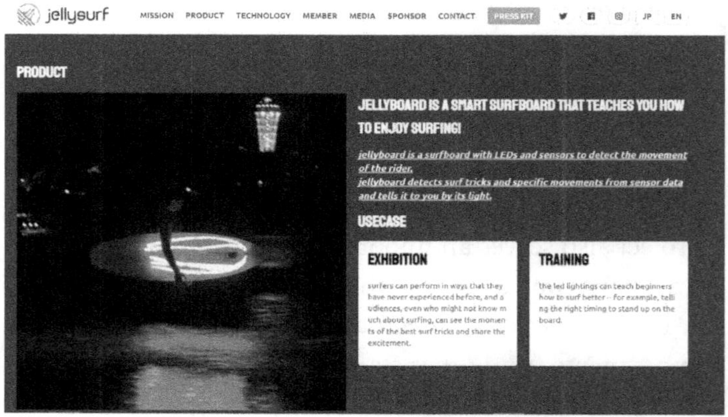

jellysurf's website

In retrospect, this social support seemed to play a crucial role in maintaining his motivation. Similarly, students at the Garage can rely on each other for the emotional support that's needed to overcome failures. For Kazme, the Garage is his home for his smart surfboard project. An angel investor provided capital for him to incorporate. He hasn't found a viable business model yet, but he actively reaches out to potential customers. After many prototypes, he has now partnered with a professional who makes boards. Maybe one day in the near future, I can introduce him to Chen of Embrace so that she can try the most recent iteration of the jellyboard. It would be a perfect topic to write about on her blog about surfing and entrepreneurship.

PART III

BEST PRACTICES FOR DESIGNING EFFECTIVE PROGRAMS AND SPACES

CHAPTER 8

ENTREPRENEURSHIP MEETS MAKER EDUCATION

—

*We're born makers. We don't just live,
but we make. We create things.*

—DALE DOUGHERTY

When was the last time you made something with your hands? If you look back on your childhood, I'm sure you played a lot, but you probably spent a lot of time making things at home and at school.

Arts and crafts was one of my favorite classes in school. I attended a public elementary school in a working-class neighborhood in Melbourne, Australia. Every school year, we would pound the clay and shape it into an object that would be fired in the kiln. I was never any good. I vividly remember making a figurine wearing a pink dress that came out looking off-kilter and had rather grotesque oval-shaped eyes. I remember because it was fun and engaging.

By college, the opportunity to make things in class virtually disappears. Creating physical prototypes and artifacts has no place in the curriculum, unless you are majoring in a discipline where production is a core activity, such as engineering, arts, design, or architecture. Although there is a push to introduce more practical, experiential ways to learn, many educators still prefer teaching theory and knowledge through traditional lecturing, especially at research universities.

Business and management departments may be the most unlikely places to be able to work with one's hands. The discipline is abstract. I struggled to see how developing business plans and ideas in class could achieve the desired outcome of developing an entrepreneurial mindset in students. In-class activities that went beyond the level of a thought experiment were few and far between.

Motivation was another formidable challenge. I'd be teaching an introduction to entrepreneurship course and more than four hundred would enroll. The overwhelming majority showed up not because they wanted to be there, but because it was mandatory. They just wanted to be done.

I spent the first five years teaching entrepreneurship with limited success. I tried to incorporate methods from Babson, MIT, Chalmers University of Technology, Stanford, and the University of Virginia. I did what was standard: project-based learning, or PBL. The students would work on a project in teams. I tried to make it as experiential as possible. I'd encourage them to get out of the classroom to interact with potential customers. I sometimes imposed a quota, telling them they had to interview five people before the next class.

The enterprising ones did go out of the building to talk to real people. They discovered something new in the process. Some came back to me later, telling me how the core concepts of entrepreneurship transformed their approach to life. It is rare that I get to hear feedback like this. Most students only take one or two of my courses during their time at the university, and I have no way of knowing how those classes impacted them later in their lives.

I was fortunate to be part of an active learning research project in which a team of education experts measured learning outcomes for my introduction course. The survey results showed a significant improvement in how students perceived their skills in communication, writing, collaboration, relationship building, time management, and leadership.

However, the researchers did not probe for changes in mindset. One of the problems in teaching entrepreneurship is that we do not yet have standard scales or methods for measuring outcomes. In our field, scholars still quarrel about the definition of entrepreneurship. Most studies in the past focused on indicators that are easiest to assess: the intent to start new businesses, for example. This does not align at all with the learning goals of my classes. Trying to convince people to start businesses is the antithesis to what I am striving to accomplish.

As far as I could see, students only seemed to learn how difficult and challenging it really was to run a business for real. Their general lack of enthusiasm stood in stark contrast with the student makers I had come to know at Kyushu University and the University of Tokyo.

By 2018, I began to sense what I was doing wrong and why. One problem was the time horizon. At Babson College, incoming students spend an entire year building out a service or product. Ours typically had only about four to six weeks to work on their projects. Most credit-bearing courses in Japan are cut up into shorter modules compared to Europe and the United States. We are also being pushed to teach in quarters rather than semesters. That means that a typical two-unit PBL course was conducted over eight weeks, including orientation and final presentations. The class met once a week for about three hours.

The other problem had to do with the learning process and the deliverables. Throughout the project, students would ideate, discuss, and analyze with sticky notes and maybe interview. But at the end of the day, they had nothing tangible to show for their work except a presentation slide deck. All bits and no atoms.

How could I infuse *making* into my courses, so that students worked with atoms, not just bits?

I began to experiment. My first thought was to bring cooking into my teaching. In her landmark article on effectuation, Sarasvathy used it as a way to distinguish between the two different logics. There are two ways a chef can organize their tasks.

In the first, the host or client picks out a menu in advance. All the chef needs to do is list the ingredients needed, shop for them, and then actually cook the meal. This is a process of causation. [146]

The second case described effectuation.

---

146 Saras D. Sarasvathy, "Causation and Effectuation: Toward a Theoretical Shift from Economic Inevitability to Entrepreneurial Contingency," *Academy of Management Review* 26, no. 2 (2001): 246.

(T)he host asks the chef to look through the cupboards in the kitchen for possible ingredients and utensils and then cook a meal. Here, the chef has to imagine possible menus based on the given ingredients and utensils, select the menu, and then prepare the meal.[147]

I recalled hearing from someone at a conference that Sarasvathy uses a kitchen for some of her classes, although I had no details. So, I improvised.

At an intensive summer course I taught in Regensburg, Germany, I designed an exercise that tasked students to cook and serve ramen, or noodles in soup, to anyone who was on campus. I handed them packs of Japanese instant noodles and ten euros to buy local ingredients.

I imposed some constraints to encourage them to practice using an effectual logic. I withheld the soup sachets that came with the package; they had to figure out a soup alternative. Each of the two teams had both Japanese and German students. Ostbayerische Technische Hochschule (OTH), the host university, gave us access to a faculty kitchen and dining room. The challenge was to somehow raise money without selling the ramen outright (which would probably have required authorization and cutting through red tape).

I only gave them a couple packs each. One team decided to create a German version, substituting the ramen noodles with Spaetzle, a traditional German pasta. They also bought a huge bag of sauerkraut, just because it was cheap.

On the day of the experiment, they went on Twitter and Facebook to reach out to both friends and strangers who might be on campus. This was summer break. Not a lot of

---

147 Sarasvathy, "Causation and Effectuation," 246.

people seemed to be around. The teams started cooking late in the morning. By lunchtime, seemingly from out of nowhere, people started coming to the communal kitchen.

The "customers" were served a bowl of ramen, showered with questions, and finally asked for a "tip." Many were more than happy to oblige.

What they learned surprised them. The students shared an assumption that their customers would value authenticity, preferring ramen that is closer to the real thing. They were wrong. The most popular version was nothing like the Japanese dish. It was the one with Spaetzle and sauerkraut.

This shocked the Japanese students. The idea to add sauerkraut came from a student from Eastern Europe who thought it would be a bit like borscht, the red beet stew. The creative twist led them to a unique insight, taking them outside the frames of their original thinking.

The ramen cooking exercise was both effective and efficient. Making things is inherently filled with uncertainty. As a consequence, small failures are inevitable. The students rebound very quickly because they are failing fast and early.

The day after, I then had the students develop a plan for creating a local ramen business. They instantly fell back to the default causal mode of thinking. They did not interview potential customers for this exercise. They did not prototype. They thought like consultants. All talk, no action.

On the final day, I listened to them present their business proposals. At least they were able to depart from the original idea (which made no sense when using the students' means at hand) and pivot. One team proposed Japanese cooking classes, for example. But they were nothing more than plans that were untested, unrealistic, and not radically interesting.

After they finished, I went over the theory of effectuation. I asked them to reflect back on the two exercises. It was at this point that they began to grasp how managerial and entrepreneurial thinking differed on a much deeper, experiential level.

Encouraged by the outcome, I tried a more ambitious experiment the following spring. A dozen Japanese students from Tokyo University of Science (TUS) traveled to Phnom Penh, Cambodia, for a four-day intensive study-abroad course in entrepreneurship. The TUS students were joined by Cambodian students studying management and business at the Royal University of Phnom Penh (RUPP).

Three teams with equal numbers of Japanese and Cambodian students were given the following challenge: to make as much money as possible in about six hours by marketing something Japanese.

Two teams decided to cook food. A third sold snacks that they brought from Japan. The two teams that cooked failed more often. In fact, one of the teams had sold nothing as of one o'clock. And when they tried selling on campus, they were promptly told by security that they did not have permission. Yet they persisted, and by the end of the day, had sold all the sweet mochi balls they had prepared in one of the student's homes.

The other team cooked Japanese Okonomiyaki pancakes. With no access to a kitchen, they staked out an area outdoors near a canteen. They bought the necessary ingredients and food packaging the previous day at a local market. One of them brought an electric grill and cooking utensils from home.

Initially, I was amused by their creativity. There was no sink, so they literally sprayed water onto a cabbage using a garden hose. But an hour later, as they began to fry the batter into pancakes, I started to panic. I picked up my phone to make a frantic call to our local coordinator. He used to own and operate a French restaurant in Tokyo and was certified as a food hygiene manager.

"Matsushita-san, I'm really worried about sanitation and that someone might get sick."

"Have they covered all the ingredients?"

I looked over, and yes, someone had covered every bowl with ingredients with a lid.

"Stop worrying. As long as they cook the pancakes so that they are well-done, they'll be fine."

I observed them more closely. It soon became clear that the emerging leader of the group—a Cambodian student— knew from experience how to keep street food safe to eat.

Of the three teams, the two that physically made something ended up learning more *and* earning more money. The one selling packaged snacks were sold out by noon. They decided not to do any more work and chose to spend the afternoon sightseeing.

Later that year, I taught what would be my last entrepreneurship course at TechShop Tokyo. Though listed as a business course, students from other departments were encouraged to audit.

The project goal was to use the digital tools at the makerspace to develop campus novelty goods that they would then actually try to sell. Over the course of two months, the students split into two teams of seven people and produced prototypes which they showed to potential customers.

The product ideas evolved into some creative prototypes, like a 3-D printed smartphone stand in the shape of a sigma (because business students see the Greek symbol all the time in their coursework); butterfly-shaped earrings cut from clear acrylic with chemical formulas etched into them; a T-shirt with a beautiful, oversized, black-and-white photo of an escalator from a well-known building on campus was produced using an extra-wide printer, a plotting machine, and a thermal press.

An idea sketch by a student of a T-shirt with a photo that doesn't look like the TUS campus on first glance

The T-shirt turned out much better than the students imagined during the initial idea sketching phase [Figure 1]. The product concept of using a hip image that didn't look like the TUS campus at a glance worked well. The cost of production was too expensive though; over thirty US dollars per shirt just for materials and printing. At least, that was their assumption after prototyping, one which they never actually tested.

In contrast, a couple weeks into the class, two students (both STEM majors) asked if they could go out and sell their prototypes. I told them they didn't need to keep coming to me for permission, but if they got into any trouble, I would take responsibility as the instructor of the class.

They had two main products. One was a plastic A4 document folder targeting physics majors. Three cute little black cats were UV printed onto the folders, along with various formulas specific to physics. Their other product was a coaster made of MDF wood. Seven interlocking parts were cut out in the form of benzine rings.

They wanted to see if they could sell to alum who were attending the upcoming Homecoming Day on campus. The event was a little over a week away.

I offered to introduce them to a senior staff member I knew who had recently transferred from our department to a marketing and public relations position. One of them met and convinced him to let her "pilot test" their products at one of the university booths.

Meanwhile, the business students worried about quality. They felt their products were not good enough to sell.

Benzine ring inspired coasters made of MDF wood using laser cutters

The coasters were very well-received by the people who came to the booth. Students loved the document folder (even though the printing was not always perfect). The pair ended up selling several hundred dollars' worth of products.

Their behavior and inclination to act rather than to wait and see left a huge impression on the others. The difference in sales—hundreds of dollars versus zero—in the course of just weeks drove home how outcomes diverge depending on a causal or effectual approach, especially in the face of uncertainty.

This course gave me two important insights. First, peer learning can be a powerful tool for breathing life into the abstract concepts we are trying to teach. Role modeling is widely recognized in the workplace as an effective developmental method for training employees. For example, it has been shown to be useful in developing ethical leadership.[148]

The Maker's Project course I taught at TechShop offered students the opportunity to observe each other in a relatively safe environment. There were no huge differences in terms of ability, seniority, and skills among them, at least in the context of the assignment. The STEM students may have perceived a lack of marketing knowledge compared to the business students. The shared experience of watching, talking, making, thinking, planning, and acting taught them more than I could ever achieve in the confines of a classroom.

The second thing I learned was the potency of physically making things. This was a class where learning from failure was explicitly embraced, even encouraged. When students created things at TechShop, they rarely got it right the first time. Working with atoms comes with more constraints than

---

148 Michael E. Brown and Linda K. Treviño, "Do Role Models Matter? An Investigation of Role Modeling as an Antecedent of Perceived Ethical Leadership," *Journal of Business Ethics* 122, no. 4 (2014).

bits. It forces students to improvise, to figure out what went wrong, and to test things over and over again until they eventually get it right. In addition, students seemed much *happier* when they were making things at TechShop than when they were doing group work in the classroom.

"Research shows that resilience can be developed through creative practice." An article in *Psychology Today*, published in June 2020 during the COVID-19 pandemic, discussed how "creativity encourages positive emotions that can unlock our inner resources for dealing with stress and uncertainty."[149]

As I introduced earlier, Barbara Fredrickson's research suggests that positive emotions encourage us to try new things and to see from a fresh perspective. These experiences build upon one another, driving both contentment and resilience.

The article referred to a study Fredrickson and her colleagues conducted in the wake of 9/11. Among the college students in New York City who were surveyed, "those who actively sought experiences that piqued their curiosity or brought them joy were less likely to be depressed than their peers who did not seek such experiences. Simultaneously, they were more likely to produce novel thought patterns when resolving challenges and find positive meaning within the problems they faced as a result of the 9/11 attack."[150]

I changed how I designed my courses after my last classes at TechShop. The practice of *making* significantly enhanced the learning experience. For nearly every entrepreneurship course I have subsequently taught, I made an effort to

---

149 Jeffrey Davis, "How Creativity Builds Resilience in Times of Crisis," *Psychology Today*, June 16, 2020.

150 Davis, "How Creativity Builds Resilience in Times of Crisis."

include at least one tangible deliverable that they have to make. Due to time constraints, most of them are in the form of bits rather than atoms. A still life photo. An app created using MIT App Inventor. A landing page. Nevertheless, they require more making than a PowerPoint presentation outlining a business idea.

My biggest success so far involves cooking. The Regensburg experiment worked because we could use a communal kitchen and dining area. Access to such facilities on campus is problematic, especially when working with dozens of people. My alternative: transform the classroom into a temporary kitchen. What we ended up doing for several programs was to use high-tech cooking appliances that were capable of preparing a full meal by plugging them into a power outlet.

An innovative machine developed by Sharp called the "Hotcook," currently available only in Japan, was perfect for our needs.[151] From the outside, the Hotcook looks like a cross between a rice cooker and a large Crock-Pot. Inside is a special mixing component that is attached to the back of the lid, which unfolds two skinny but durable arms that automatically stir the ingredients in the inner pot. With this additional feature, entire repertoires of dishes that previously required several manual steps could be combined and executed automatically.

Embedded sensors help control temperature and pressure. Hotcook uses no open flames, and the lid is closed during cooking, making it fireproof and safe. Desks can easily be used as tabletops for chopping and cutting. Most classrooms

---

151 "ヘルシオホットクック(Healsio Hotcook)," on Sharp's website, accessed

October 13, 2020.

have running water somewhere nearby where food and dishes can be washed.

Each team was given a Hotcook, an operating manual, and a cookbook. Random ingredients and utensils were laid out on a table. "You have two hours to cook dinner for your team members. Ready, go!" Since the choice of food and seasonings are limited, the students quickly discover that they cannot use the recipes in the cookbook. They had to cook effectually.

Students open Sharp's Hotcook cooking machine to check on their vegetarian dish

This workshop is based on a more elaborate one that Sarasvathy and her colleagues conduct at conferences and for corporate clients. A restaurant is rented out for the evening. Participants cook using the commercial kitchen, professional appliances, and utensils of the restaurant. Upward of sixty people split into a dozen teams to prepare either an appetizer, main course, or dessert to feed everyone.

I've attended two such workshops. Both evenings were amazing experiences. The dishes were creative, spontaneous, and reflected the diverse culinary backgrounds of those participating. The conversations over dinner were also lively and engaging.

In a matter of hours, communal cooking brings people physically and psychologically closer. The experience is shared, so it is easier to have discussions in a debrief that usually follows the next day. It also enabled us to run through most of the core principles of effectuation in a condensed time frame. We got to learn from unexpected failures and co-creation with others. We had to focus on the means at hand and the resources we were able to control.

The Hotcook is also useful for demonstrating causation. On the last day of a program, I brought the appliance to the classroom, with enough pre-cut ingredients to serve the students in the class. The students were asked to make curry, one of the most popular dishes in the Hotcook recipe book. They read the instructions, put the ingredients in the pot, chose the settings, and then hit the start button. All in all, this took about fifteen minutes max.

Then, we left the machines to do their thing. I asked them to reflect upon the communal cooking on the first day. How did it contrast to the cooking that they just did? Did it feel different? All the students said that the effectual cooking was much more fun, emotional, and social. It was more creative and even innovative.

This kind of action-based, experiential learning is many times more effective in teaching the principles of effectuation than straight lecturing. It is more memorable too. I have yet to figure out how to scale the cooking workshop to my larger classes, which sometimes have over two hundred students. We'd need at least forty Hotcook machines as well as multiple classrooms. But for more intimate classes, the exercise works well, with the added bonus of being able to enjoy a meal afterward.

Even after seven years of teaching entrepreneurship, I am still only scratching the surface of how to integrate maker education into what I do. I was motivated to write this book because I wanted to uncover some of the best practices that other people have figured out through their programs. In the final chapter, I will share what I have been able to dig up through my reporting on Hongo Tech Garage and their incubation programs.

CHAPTER 9

BEST PRACTICES FOR CAMPUS MAKERSPACES

*The achievements we savor most start
with a struggle and end with hard-earned
mastery. Success tastes sweeter—and
becomes more repeatable—when it's
the product of deliberate practice.*

—ADAM GRANT

At the heart of innovation is new combinations.[152] Amazon brought the Internet to retail. Google applied the structure of academic citations to web searches. Netflix used algorithms to calculate what combinations of directors and actors could produce the next blockbuster movie.

---

152 Joseph Schumpeter, *Theory of Economic Development* (Routledge, 2017).

The most disruptive innovations nearly always start with an industry outsider who tinkers with novel combinations of technology, resources, processes, and business models.

Clayton Christensen wrote an entire book about the innovator's dilemma. His disruption theory describes the process of how David beats Goliath in industry. As incumbent businesses "focus on improving their products and services for their most demanding (and usually most profitable) customers, they exceed the needs of some segments and ignore the needs of others. Entrants that prove disruptive begin by successfully targeting those overlooked segments, gaining a foothold by delivering more-suitable functionality—frequently at a lower price."[153]

Higher education is in the midst of a major disruption. The COVID-19 pandemic is putting unprecedented pressure on those of us in this industry to reevaluate how we can effectively provide education and research in the twenty-first century. It is clear that online learning will transform university classrooms.

The stories in this book give us a glimpse of a different kind of disruption: the emergence of an entrepreneurial university. In the future that has already happened, students, not faculty, are driving innovation and research. They are the ones who are serious about solving the wicked, systemic problems of the world. They are showing us that it is not just about the science and technology, but also about practicing how to shape, craft, and validate novel solutions that people actually want and need.

---

153   Clayton M. Christensen, Michael E. Raynor, and Rory McDonald, "What Is Disruptive Innovation?," *Harvard Business Review*, December 2015.

If I were still a reporter and had to identify one individual to feature as a disruptive entrepreneur in higher education, it would most certainly be Takaaki Umada, founder of Hongo Tech Garage. The student-driven innovations showcased in this book did not occur in a vacuum. In this chapter, I will identify the best practices that have emerged through the endeavors of people like Umada and his team at the Garage. I hope they will be useful for people interested in designing and running makerspaces on-campus that enable students to innovate.

Umada is the ultimate outsider, perfectly positioned to shake up the status quo. For one thing, he had never gone to college in Japan. He majored in cognitive and computer science at the University of Toronto in Canada.

Second, his industry experience at a "gaishikei (foreign)" company was like water and oil in the context of a Japanese institution in higher education.

After graduation, he returned to Japan to work for Microsoft, initially as a product manager for Visual Studio and Azure. He talked about the insane hours he would spend at work, just like I did when I was at Nikkei in my twenties. Later, he evangelized Microsoft technologies like the Kinect, and eventually worked with startups as part of the company's accelerator programs.[154]

After nearly eight years, he left Microsoft and went on a personal sabbatical.[155] In early summer of 2016, a project he was working on fell through. He took an offer to develop a

---

154   "馬田 隆明 (Umada Takaaki)," *FastGrow*, June 28, 2019.

155   "執筆者情報 馬田 隆明 (Author Information Takaaki Umada)", Biz/
      Zine.

new platform for supporting startups and entrepreneurship at the University of Tokyo.

The Japanese financial firm Daiwa Securities Group Inc. had just committed to a significant gift that would fund programs and a makerspace for the next few years. [156] The university was looking for somebody to run the initiative.

Among the many things that inspire me about Umada as an entrepreneurship educator is how he practiced what he preached. He operated using lean startup principles: build, measure, learn.[157] As soon as he was hired, he immediately went into action. His first order of business was to find a location for the makerspace.

Less than a month later, he signed a lease to occupy the second floor of an office building, right across the street from the Hongo campus. It was only seconds away from the famed "Akamon (Red Gate)" where tourists take photos to commemorate their visit to the most prestigious university in Japan.

It was critically important both operationally and symbolically for the makerspace to be close, but nevertheless off-campus. That way, they would not be bogged down with university rules that could be detrimental to student and startup success.

He also interviewed his customers. Over the course of a month, Umada spoke to over fifty students to probe for their

---

156 The University of Tokyo and Daiwa Securities Group Inc., "東京大学と大和証券グループによる産学連携「東京大学本郷テックガレージ（大和証券グループ寄附プロジェクト）」を設置," News Release, September 9, 2016.

157 Eric Ries, *The Lean Startup: How Today's Entrepreneurs Use Continuous Innovation to Create Radically Successful Businesses* (New York: Crown Business, 2011).

wants and needs. "I would take them to Starbucks and buy them a drink," he said.

This led him to a unique insight that would drive the physical look and feel of the makerspace.

Umada wanted to create a place that would serve as a base camp for students who liked to engineer and tinker. It had to be welcoming for people like Steve Wozniak, not Steve Jobs. This was why he was talking only to technical types who were active in clubs like "RoboTech" or had been contestants for the Todai To Texas (TTT) competition.

They made one thing absolutely clear. "Please don't make the space *hip*."

This was the year that TechShop Tokyo opened. Co-working spaces were popping up across the city, many of them designed to look cool.

Such stylish places did not feel welcoming to an engineering student, and they would hesitate to go in. They also said they wanted to distance themselves from the "business types" who were only in it for the money and exploited people like themselves. Making money was neither a worthy nor noble cause for them.

Hence, the space was named the Hongo Tech Garage, a secret base where students have the freedom to work on technical projects that *they* initiated, not their professors or supervisors. It would be equipped with hand tools, digital fabrication equipment, design software, and computational resources, so that they can rapidly move from idea to prototype to deployment in both hardware and software-based projects.

Every time I have asked university administrators to consider creating a makerspace on campus, I inevitably get the same answer: we already have those machines, so why can't the students use those? The reality is that it is almost impossible for students from another department to use them. Kyushu University's Joshua Lawn found this out the hard way when he knocked on the doors of every place that had the tools he needed at the new Ito campus. They mostly said no, and so he had to find loopholes in the system to gain access.

Umada wanted to co-create the makerspace with the students. He selected a small group to advise him on everything from what equipment to buy to the layout of the floor. They decided what brand, what model, and what kind of machines and tools they would want to use.

Katsufumi Matsui, who was later hired to run the Garage, told me that they took extra care in selecting which soldering tools to buy. They went to an online specialty store for hand tools, MonotaRO, and chose the most expensive ones. The stations and irons added up to over 100,000 yen (1,000 US dollars). "It was one of the best investments we made because the students solder all the time," said Matsui.

The shop floor takes up only a fraction of the Garage. "It's probably too small," admitted Umada. It is functional and well-utilized, fulfilling Umada's requirement that people can go back and forth between making prototypes and discussions.

The machines with the heaviest usage include the 30-watt laser cutter and the 3-D printers (Form 2, Up300 and UP Box+). In contrast, the hand tools for woodworking are rarely used. The CNC milling machine (KitMill SR420) gets no usage at all. It is often faster, cheaper, and more reliable to outsource metal parts to specialized companies rather than spend countless hours manning the machine.

The rest of the floor is mostly filled with movable tables and chairs where students spend most of their time discussing and working on their projects. Whenever there are lectures and presentations, they clear the central area of furniture and sit on the floor to listen.

There is a cooking, eating, and lounging area on the opposite end, as well as a small but carefully curated collection of books on business, design, and technology. Trophies and award banners won by Garage members are displayed along one small section of the wall.

The Garage's relaxation corner lined with tatami mats

Matsui walked me over towards the entrance of the shop floor. "This may be the most important part of the Garage," he said, as he pointed to a series of steel shelves that were all stabilized with spring tension rods to prevent them from toppling during earthquakes. "Storage space for projects," he explained. It mattered to students to be able to leave their prototypes and other random things at the Garage. Every project is allocated its own space.

The Garage admitted its first batch of students on August 1, only weeks after the lease contract was signed. Umada called the sessions the Summer Founder's Program (SFP) as a tribute to Y Combinator's original name when it launched in Boston in 2005. [158] Umada hoped that, someday, a team from the Garage would be chosen to go through the YC acceleration program.

Their primary financial function is to provide funding for implementing projects.

YC has been wildly successful in incubating high-growth startups. Dropbox, Airbnb, Stripe, and Reddit to name a few. It was an investment fund from its inception and "represents the union of two ideas that had not previously been combined: the application of mass production techniques to startup funding." It is not only more efficient to produce startups in "batches," but also beneficial for the founders too.[159] In 2019, the top 101 companies the program had funded out of a total of over 2000 had a cumulative valuation of a whopping 155 *billion* US dollars.[160]

"We started this by accident, and never realized it would become as big as it has," said Jessica Livingston in an episode of *Startup School Radio*.[161] She and her co-founder and husband, Paul Graham, were dating at the time. Livingston was

---

158   Alyson Shontell, "Paul Graham Founded Y Combinator 7 Years Ago to Create a Job for His Wife," *Business Insider*, March 18, 2012.

159   Paul Graham et al., "Y Combinator's Founding Principles," *Y Combinator* (blog), October, 2017.

160   Greg Kumparak, "These Are the Top Y Combinator Companies of All Time, Based on Valuation," *TechCrunch*, October 2, 2019.

161   "Jessica Livingston on the Accidental Origin of Y Combinator," *Y Combinator* (blog), November 25, 2015.

bored with her job at an investment bank in Boston and was about to quit to write a book about startup founders.

"We just spent a lot of our time talking about what was broken. What was broken at the time was that there was no standardized and branded source of seed funding," said Livingston. Many of the people establishing startups were programmers and their ventures didn't need a lot of capital. She continued.

(T)he option if you were just wanting to get into first gear of your startup, you'd have to find some rich relative or friend who would give you some money. And after that, the next option really was venture capitalists, and they wanted to put millions of dollars into the company. And we thought, "Gosh, there's really this void of a place you can to and get a small amount of funding to help you live and pay your expenses and build the product. [162]

Therefore, they created an investment company, developed an application process, and called for college students to join them. They began with two hundred thousand dollars, including investments from two other founders.

Graham didn't take the first summer program seriously. "That's one of the reasons we especially like funding ideas that might be dismissed as 'toys'—because YC itself was dismissed as one initially," wrote Graham in a blog post chronicling how the accelerator started.[163]

---

162 "Jessica Livingston."

163 Paul Graham, "How Y Combinator Started," *Paul Graham* (blog), March, 2012.

SFP at the University of Tokyo differs from its namesake in several ways. Most importantly, the program is not in the business of getting startups off the ground. The goal of SFP, according to Umada, is to allow students to practice entrepreneurship so that they may be better positioned to launch a startup in ten years' time. The university does not ask for an equity stake in startups that happen to come out of the program.

Nevertheless, Umada borrowed many of YC's founding principles when designing SFP. It puts the students' interests first "before even our own."[164] An extension of this principle is the rule of prohibiting grown-ups (we call them "shakai-jin," which literally means "people from society") from entering the premises.

Co-working spaces intended for students are sometimes teeming with "shakai-jin" who mean well but end up domineering. The best way to prevent this is to keep them out. Exceptions are made only for mentoring sessions, invited speakers, and judges for demo day and final presentations.

SFP participants are advised and persuaded but never commanded. According to YC's founding principles, "since you can't know what it's like to start a startup without having done it, those who advise the founders should be mostly people who have."[165] This is why the program chooses alum from the startup community as mentors. They usually steer away from academics and corporate types.

The startup culture is everything. "YC has to be fast, cheap, informal, and focused on essentials. If something

---

164   Graham et al. "Founding Principles."

165   Graham et al. "Founding Principles."

seems like the sort of bullshit a big company would engage in, it's probably a mistake."[166]

Finally, the "most successful founders are motivated less by money than by a consuming interest in what they're building."[167] The Garage generally does not accept applicants who don't have the desire or inclination to actually make things. Students who want to found startups because they want to get rich need not apply. Aspiring strategic management consultants with elaborate business plans will also be screened out.

The Garage explicitly rejects business-oriented projects, services with no technology element, products based on imaginary users and imaginary needs, and media art that has no customers.

Here are the types of ideas it is willing to support according to its website:

- An idea that a few users fall deeply in love with (including one that you yourself really desire) rather than an idea that lots of users like.
- An idea that solves a problem you have, or someone close to you has.
- An idea that was not possible before, but now is.
- An idea that nobody has ever heard or seen, rather than one that is straightforward.
- Something that is differentiated or novel compared to the past.
- An idea that challenges new frontiers, something that is slightly offbeat compared to what is currently trendy. [168]

---

166 Graham et al. "Founding Principles."

167 Graham et al. "Founding Principles."

168 "Project 募集するプロジェクトについて (About Our Call for Projects)," on Hongo Tech Garage's website, accessed October 13, 2020.

Here are some other "hacks" and best practices that have emerged out of the Garage in my words (not theirs):

- Innovation as a SIDE PROJECT
  - The last two words are capitalized on purpose. We have to be *very* careful not to lose sight of the students' primary objective: to study toward a degree. Projects at the Garage are at best a "gig," not a life commitment. Research shows that hybrid entrepreneurs—people who don't give up their day jobs to start a new business—are much more likely to succeed in their ventures, so we should expect the same for students.[169]

- Safeguarding student freedom
  - Provide protection from the outside world to give students a space to play and practice. This is arguably the single most important role that Umada and Matsui play at the Garage. The "no adults" rule is but one of the manifestations. Others include establishing procedures for spending project money that are flexible yet appropriate and responsible, as well as incorporating security systems that minimize the trade-off between access and safety.

- Make or die
  - The official mantra of SFP is deploy or die. But you have to have a prototype before you can deploy. Unless you can make one (or at least willing to try),

---

169 Stuart Read et al., *Effectual Entrepreneurship* (London and New York: Routledge/Taylor & Francis Group, 2017).

you will probably be screened out during the application process.

- Students are accountable for learning how to make
  - There simply isn't enough time to teach students how to make. The university offers many pathways for learning to use digital fabrication machines, including through formal classes.

- Deadlines, deadlines, deadlines!
  - The definition of a project is that it has a beginning and an end. Deadlines and milestones drive activity in between and are important motivators for students to get things done.

- Quantify and monitor student activity levels
  - Throughout the entire eight weeks, SFP teams fill out a form online to log the hours they spent coding and interviewing customers each week. The data is shared with everyone. The outcomes of teams with higher activity levels are *always superior*. The students can see the difference on the final day of presentations.

- Go, no-go decisions driven by competitions
  - Both summer and spring programs encourage students to compete in competitions such as Todai To Texas and MITOU. If they want to continue working on their projects after the program ends, there is also the option to apply for "gap" project funding through the Garage in anticipation of participating in those competitions in the future. These serve as external validation of the project, helping students

judge whether they ought to continue or to kill their project.

- Three strikes and you're in
  - Anecdotal evidence suggests that students often go through three failures before getting to a viable opportunity. In their first try, they make something that they personally want. This one fails because no one else wants it. Next, they make something for others, but the product doesn't solve a real problem. On their third try, they get to a unique insight that gets them to product-solution fit.

- Support both hardware *and* software projects
  - While the Garage focuses primarily on physical products, it also welcomes software projects too. Such teams learn from the hardware types and vice versa. Business ideas based on bits are easier and faster to deploy and are more likely to launch as real ventures quickly, helping to motivate and inspire others.

- Students raise cash through grants and scholarships, not investments
  - One significant advantage students have over other entrepreneurs is access to grants and scholarships to fund their projects. The MITOU program is just one example of a recurring funding opportunity that privileges students. Although applicants don't have to be enrolled at a university, Garage members have a significant leg up because they can tap into the knowledge and experience base built up from previous cohorts. As a result, their application forms and

presentations are polished and have a higher chance of being accepted.

- Projects can also be positioned as scientific research and be eligible for grants, especially if it is linked to a doctoral degree. The Garage provides additional project money, which functions a bit like gap funding for startups. The net result is that students can secure "working capital" without incorporating and giving up equity to investors.

- Alumni as mentors and partners
  - The Garage and SFP benefit tremendously from the rich network of alumni who can serve as mentors and partners for student projects. They are very selective about who they ask to support the students, however.

- For the students, by the students
  - The Garage hires students to run the day-to-day operations of the makerspace. Most of them have gone through SFP, and those who haven't often can't help themselves from signing up. Many successful applicants to TTT and MITOU return to SFP to give tips on pitching, producing promotional videos, and putting together strong grant applications.
  - On Slack and other platforms, students post their personal best practices, configurations, and settings for machines, code, project management tips, and other information and knowledge that they feel would benefit others. Even after they graduate, members continue to have access to the Slack workspace and sometimes jump into conversations. Over time, a strong community of practice develops.

- Staff who can code
    - It helps to have a full-time staff who can code. Toshinari Shimokawa, who helps Matsui manage the Garage, is a programmer, and he developed the custom program for the entry and security system. He also wrote a simple application for checking out books using Slack. Deploy or die culture extends to the Garage staff, generating small but meaningful innovations that enhance productivity, efficiency, communication, and knowledge transfer.

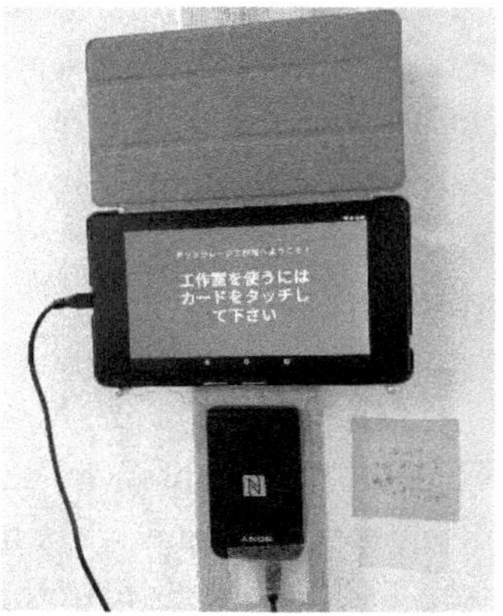

Customized entry system to the shop floor

The overarching principle that governs the Garage is its focus on students, not startups. When the University of Tokyo launched its first entrepreneurship course in 2005, one of the outcomes it evaluated was the number of companies founded by students.[170] More startups implied that

---

170   Katsuya Hasegawa, *Startups 101* (Tokyo: University of Tokyo Press, 2019).

the program was better. Veteran educators know this to be wrong.

At the United States Association for Small Business and Entrepreneurship's annual conference in 2020, several speakers referred to the danger of looking at the number of student startups as indicators of success. Such an approach is fraught with conflicts of interest that may do more harm than good.

Not that the Garage holds back anyone from trying. One software startup that came out of SFP is Mantra, which developed an intelligent, automated translation platform specifically for manga and graphic novels.

The company was founded by two PhD students: Shonosuke Ishiwatari, who specialized in machine translation and natural language processing, and Ryota Hinami, who researched image recognition.

During its project phase, the team raised about 15 million yen (150,000 US dollars), not from investors, but from awards and grants alone. They raised an additional 18 million yen (180,000 US dollars) in grant money after they incorporated. Early project funds enabled them to buy a huge manga database which they used to train their artificial intelligence (AI) engine. The platform they developed not only automatically generates high quality translations by using AI, but also lays out text in the right dialogue bubble in the correct order, saving enormous amounts of time and labor.

Both founders are on track to graduate with their PhDs. Shonosuke, the CEO, was planning to be a researcher. One day, in his final year as a PhD student, he heard an alum speak as a guest lecturer. He was four years his senior, and had founded Elephantech, a startup known for its technology printing circuitry onto paper using silver ink.

"What he was basically saying was, it's not as though you're going to die drowning in debt because you founded a startup. You have the chance to do something epoch-making!" The talk opened Shonosuke's eyes. "I couldn't do this alone. I was thinking, who could I ask?" Then, on his way home, in the heat of the moment, he LINE messaged Ryota.

"I have something I want to ask you about my research," he entered, which, of course, was just a charade. He was going to ask him to come work with him on Mantra. Ryota said yes, but only as a side project. However, he eventually decided to go all in. After graduating, they moved from the Garage to FoundX, the incubation program for alumni, launched and currently run by Umada. They incorporated in January 2020 and raised 80 million yen in their first round of funding from investors.[171]

Umada dreams of the day a startup born from SFP is accepted into the YC program. Mantra is the closest so far.

"When we launched, I set a target to generate one hundred projects per year by year three," said Umada. He seemed disappointed that they haven't hit those goals yet. But after interacting with many students at the Garage, I feel that Umada may be underestimating the impact his vision and leadership is having.

After finishing the interviews for this book, I noticed something interesting. As educators, we fully expect that some of the students who go through our programs who never intended to start companies change their minds and end up doing so. This is why the outcome most often measured to assess the efficacy of such programs is

---

171 Mantra, "世界のマンガファンにリアルタイムで多言語配信、マンガAI翻訳のMantraが資金調達を実施," *PR Times*, June 8, 2020.

entrepreneurial intentions (EI), or how much someone is thinking about starting a business.[172] I've noted earlier that researchers have begun shifting away from focusing on EI because we are trying to develop entrepreneurial mindsets, not startup founders.

What we may still be overlooking is how great programs and communities like SFP and the Garage in higher education can be catalysts for transformation in the opposite direction: students choosing to pursue academic research over starting companies, at least in the short run. All three students from the Garage featured in Part II are currently doctoral students engaged in rigorous research.

Mako, for example, decided not to continue with her breakfast robot. She is now researching how 3-D printers can be used to design and produce innovative food. She never imagined herself co-authoring scholarly papers with one of the professors who mentored her at Teatime Hackathon Lab where she began honing her programming skills. Kazme is being supervised by Jun Rekimoto, one of the university's most famous faculty in information sciences, who also holds a position at Sony Computer Sciences Laboratories. He researches human-computer interaction based on his intelligent surfboard. Masaki continues to be driven by purpose and is engaged in research that will further enhance the capabilities of artificial voice boxes.

Management scholars recognize the power of transformational leadership in organizations, in which a leader "identifies the needed change, creates a vision to guide the

---

172   Alexandros Kakouris and Panagiotis Georgiadis, "Analysing Entrepreneurship Education: A Bibliometric Survey Pattern," *Journal of Global Entrepreneurship Research* 6, no. 1 (February 2016).

change through inspiration, and executes the change with the commitment of the members of the group." [173] At its best, entrepreneurship education can also transform individuals, to enable them to become innovation makers. Campus makerspaces in particular can empower students with technical skills, science, and effectual mindsets that form the foundation for making a difference in the world. Seeing these emerging innovators learn, fail, and grow has been a source of great optimism in these challenging times. Focus on students, and everything else will follow.[174]

---

173   Business Dictionary, s.v. "transformational leadership," accessed October 13, 2020; Bernard M. Bass and Ronald E. Riggio, *Transformational Leadership* (Mahwah, N.J.: L. Erlbaum Associates, 2006).

174   The original YC founding principles substituted founders for students. See Graham et al. "Y Combinator's Founding Principles."

EPILOGUE

In the fall of 2019, Sunao Hiruta, an assistant professor in design at Shinshu University, came to TechShop Tokyo to help me teach the Maker's Project course for students at Tokyo University of Science. Over lunch, he began telling me about a cool project he was working on with a small regional confectioner. Shinshu University is in Nagano, a region famous for its natural beauty and produce. Hiruta was asked to help the company redesign a traditional Japanese delicacy called yokan, a type of sweet and dense jelly that is usually made of red beans.

Their yokan was unusual. It was made from locally grown persimmons, the orange-colored fruit that comes into season in autumn. They were looking to innovate how they sold it. Yokan traditionally comes in large rectangular blocks, about three centimeters tall and fifteen centimeters long. The "cloyingly sticky" jelly is sliced into serving-size pieces. [175] Their idea was to sell a single-portion version, like sticks of string

---

175   Audrey Foo, "5 Scary Japanese Foods and Why You Should Try Them," *Japan Today,* August 19, 2018.

cheese. They would target domestic Japanese tourists visiting Nagano.

There was a hitch though. The minimum for a custom packaging order was ten thousand pieces. This was a huge risk for a product that had yet to be proven in the market.

Hiruta came up with a workaround made possible by the maker revolution. If they used a digital cutting machine called a plotter in combination with a color laser printer, they could not only easily prototype many designs, but also produce commercial-grade packaging in small batches.

In theory, this sounded great. In practice, getting the perforations right became a major design challenge. It took many iterations to get to a package that would easily tear both the outside cardboard and the inner plastic wrapper at the same time.

The redesign was stylish and also told the story behind the product. It went on to be a commercial success. Given the production volume, Hiruta assumed they would contract out the packaging as usual. "I was stunned when I visited them some time later to discover they were *still* using the same printer and plotter, even though the product was selling," said Hiruta. The sweets maker decided to continue making the packaging on their own, partly to retain flexibility. "They could produce hundreds of pieces in their downtime, so they decided not to bother going to the printers."

Desktop publishing software gave offices and homes a turnkey printing press for documents. Hiruta's experience suggests that packaging is about to undergo a similar disruption. Prices for design software have come down to about sixty dollars per license. These applications have enough features and functionality to be a viable alternative to professional applications like Adobe Illustrator.

Digital cutting machines are also cheaper and more accessible. Unlike laser cutters that are still too expensive for individuals and small businesses, the industrial-grade plotter Hiruta used in his Yokan project was an entry-level model priced at around fifteen hundred US dollars. Cutting machines for the home have a price point of less than four hundred US dollars and have become wildly popular among DIY types and women who like handcrafting.

Hiruta collaborated with the sweets maker as part of a design research project. It piqued my interest because the problem he had solved for the local business is one that is shared by many small and medium-sized businesses in the food industry.

I was reminded of a corporate partner we had worked with for another course in innovation I was co-teaching at Hiroshima University, my new home. Hirotuku was a local family business that produced tsukudani, a savory, kombu-based rice topping. The students in the class were tasked with proposing new ways to increase online sales. They kept coming back to the notion of updating packaging to appeal to a younger, more international generation of customers. They didn't have time to do any prototyping, though, so the idea didn't go anywhere.

A couple months after the course ended, I met with the Hirotuku president, Arata Takemoto, to follow up on a student proposal to renew their website. I casually asked him a question about packaging. "Do you suffer from the wall of ten thousand?" I asked. Despite the cryptic question, Takemoto knew exactly what I was referring to.

"Yes, yes, we do. You're talking about the minimum lot size, right? We waste so much packaging because of the ten thousand minimum."

Food businesses that distribute to supermarkets and other retail outlets are notorious for the number of SKUs, or Stock Keeping Units, they have to provide for what is essentially the same product. Retailers often demand customized packaging. That means Hirotuku has to buy at least ten thousand pieces for each different design. The minimum lot size was not just a cost issue, but also an environmental one. Takemoto felt guilty for having to throw out so many unused boxes and packets each year. I told him about Hiruta's experiment with the yokan. He said he was very interested, and that if I ever organized a workshop about this, he would gather some of his industry peers who would also likely want to participate.

Universities in the twenty-first century are increasingly being called to go beyond their primary roles in education and research. They are being asked to collaborate more with other stakeholders in industry and society in order to use research outcomes to solve real-life problems. In this context, higher education has a role to play in helping consumers and businesses adopt the new digital fabrication technologies that are driving the maker revolution.

Hiruta and his colleague at Shinshu University, Hiroyuki Muramatsu, who specializes in technology education, have been extremely active in reaching out to the community. Muramatsu spearheaded a research project with a local company that provided the seed funding for a Fab Lab they created from scratch on campus. To save money, pretty much everything in the space, including shelving and tables, was handmade with the students. Much of what I learned about digital fabrication, I owe to Muramatsu and Hiruta, whom I initially met through TechShop. I attended a hackathon they had organized with the city of Sakakimachi and local executives to develop new product concepts that tourists would want to buy.

Muramatsu was the one who opened me up to the possibilities of bringing maker technologies into the classroom. The same students who had struggled with generating business ideas flourished in his prototyping workshop, which took advantage of circuit boards and programming tools developed for children. Their creativity was unleashed and harnessed when they worked with their hands and tinkered. The emerging ideas were much more novel and innovative.

The packaging workshop has yet to happen because I took a fork in the road. At an academic conference in early 2020, I discovered a course on content entrepreneurship taught by Eric Koester at Georgetown University.

At the outset of the workshop introducing the course, Koester said something that made me sit up in my seat. He talked about how close he had come to giving up teaching entrepreneurship altogether. I could completely relate to his frustration that, despite the excitement and engagement in the classroom, his students did not seem to *do* anything after the course ended. What was the point?

Koester dug deeply into his own experiences as a serial entrepreneur. The one that stood out was transformational. It had to do with startups, but in a slightly tangential way. It was his experience writing books including his first, *What Every Engineer Should Know About Starting a High-Tech Business Venture.*

As a last-ditch effort, he decided to test a wild idea. What if he had students write and publish a book to experience entrepreneurship? This made perfect sense to me. Book writing is about *making* something. It was much more tangible and physical than a business proposal. Koester applied lean startup practices to the writing and publishing processes. This also made sense because it would increase the odds of success.

Koester's experiment went phenomenally well. It was as if he had swung and hit a home run with bases fully loaded. After several iterations, he was able to scale the course so that he could teach more than two hundred students per cohort. An innovative book production model emerged, enabling nearly all of them to become published authors. What's more, they learned the lean startup method *experientially* without even knowing it.

I felt as though I had discovered the Holy Grail. I've always had an inferiority complex teaching entrepreneurship because I had no practical experience in startups. Koester's program would enable me to work from my strengths as a former working journalist. It was also a disruptive innovation that had the potential to transform the publishing industry. "I have to bring this to Japan," I thought.

That's why I signed up to write a book. I began taking Koester's weekly classes online via Zoom on Fridays at seven in the morning Japan time. This was my chance to experience what it was like to work on a startup while simultaneously getting a book out, something I had been thinking about for years. I could see how my first draft was a Minimum Viable Product, or MVP. It had barely enough words to make the cut and was basically an assortment of stories rather than a manuscript.

My two editors were my mentors who helped me stay motivated and on track. The crowdsourcing campaign forced me to create customers long before the product was finished. I tapped into my network of colleagues, classmates, and business partners, the people I know, and was overwhelmed by their warm support, enthusiasm, and commitment to buy the book. As I rushed to finish the manuscript, I was constantly fighting against the urge to strive for perfection. Getting a product to market is more important, I kept reminding myself.

In the famous 2005 commencement speech at Stanford, Steve Jobs said, "You can't connect the dots looking forward; you can only connect them looking backward."[176] When I look backward from this book project, the first dot can be traced to a classroom at Georgetown University. This was 1991. The first Gulf war had just erupted, and I was taking organizational behavior taught by a young professor with ginger hair. This was my first management course ever and it left an impression because we did many hands-on exercises, including some using Tinkertoys.

The paper I wrote on creativity for that class has been in my keepsake box for nearly thirty years. In it, I argued that we tend to think we are not creative if we are not good at art. "Perhaps this misunderstanding comes from the word itself, for the word implies that you must create something in order to be creative. Creating is only one element of creativity. The main point is to do something that is different or unique, to give whatever you are doing a certain twist to it."

Trying to understand the nature of how and why people create new things has been the driving force of much of the work I have done since. There is some truth to what I wrote as a college student, but the full answer still eludes me.

I kept the paper because it helped boost my confidence at a time when, as an international exchange student from

---

176 Steve Jobs, ""You've Got to Find What You Love," Jobs Says," *Stanford News*, 2005.

Japan, I felt I wasn't good enough compared to the witty, intelligent classmates around me. At the end of the paper, the professor wrote in green ink, "Emi, good job. (A) thoughtful, insightful analysis," signed with illegible initials.

During one of Koester's classes, a student mentioned in a breakout session that the founder of our publishing company, Brian Bies, went to Georgetown, and his father was a professor there too. I had met Bies at the conference and knew that he had taken Koester's class, and went on to establish New Degree Press in order to support the new publishing model. His father, I learned from the student, taught leadership and management.

Suddenly, it clicked. After class, I pulled out a box that has moved with me from Tokyo to California to Fukuoka back to Tokyo and now sat in my closet in Hiroshima. Inside, along with my master's thesis and primary school project books, was my creativity paper. It was dated January 31, 1991, written for Professor Bies. Robert Bies, my instructor, was Brian's father.

The dots connected; I had come full circle. The classes I took at Georgetown such as History of Jazz I & II, Art History, Constitutional Law, Shakespeare, and of course Management and Organizational Behavior, were not only unforgettable, but have had a lasting impact on who I am today. It seems like fate to have the privilege of taking one more so many years later.

While writing this book, I also discovered something new about Doris Drucker's favorite Yogiism. Apparently, the fork in the road existed. [177] It didn't matter which one you took. Either way, you ended up at Yogi Berra's house.

177 Kate Zernike, "A New Jersey Township Mourns Yogi Berra, Its Civic Treasure," *New York Times*, September 23, 2015.

ACKNOWLEDGMENTS

Taking a fork to embark on this adventure felt like a leap of faith. I was in New Orleans for the annual conference of the United States Association of Small Business and Entrepreneurship (USASBE), running on the treadmill at the gym in my hotel early in the morning and debating in my mind about whether I should do this or not. By the time I went back to my room, I knew I had to take the fork.

This book could not have been conceived without USASBE and the community of educators and professionals that supports the association. I attended the conference expecting to get feedback for a research project, and came home with a commitment to become a student in Eric Koester's content entrepreneurship course (a.k.a. the Book School) to publish a book in English by Christmas. Thank you, Eric, for letting me participate in the program. I hope that one day, I can bring what you do to Japan.

Cindy Sherman, I would not be at USASBE if it weren't for you. I cherish our friendship and hope we will continue having fun.

I stand on the shoulders of many great people who have inspired, enlightened and motivated me. I dedicate this book to my dear mentor, Joseph A. Maciariello, who supervised my dissertation and taught me so much about Peter Drucker's body of work. Sadly, he passed away shortly after I completed my first draft. Joe is my ultimate role model in academia. I miss you and hope I can pay forward what you gave to me.

A huge thank-you to my colleagues at the University of Tokyo—Katsuya Hasegawa, Takaaki Umada, Katsufumi Matsui, and Toshinari Shimokawa—for graciously giving me access to Hongo Tech Garage and the amazing students there. I am particularly grateful to Katsufumi for being my sounding board and for helping me at every step of the book writing process. I am excited for the opportunity to work with all of you on the research projects that are coming. In addition, I would like to extend my gratitude to Shigeo Kagami. I deeply respect your vision, leadership, and dedication to entrepreneurship education at Todai and in Japan.

I would also like to acknowledge the amazing people I have had the pleasure of working with in entrepreneurship education at various stages of my fledgling academic career. They include Michael Cusumano, Seiichiro Hangai, Jun Tsusaka, Yuichi Katayori, Sam Nakane, Soichiro Okamura, Himeka Ijuin, Junichi Shimada, Hiroaki Fujikawa, Hitotora Higashikuni, Hideo Kudo, Nozomi Enomoto, Satoka Yamane, Mariko Watanabe, Satoshi Takahashi, Masahiro Naito, and Masaaki Takei from my brief tenure at the Tokyo University of Science; Hiromi Yamada, Megumi Takata, Shingo Igarashi, Hirofumi Taniguchi, Chihaya Adachi, and Toru Tanigawa from my time at Kyushu University; and my wonderful new colleagues at Hiroshima University, with a special shout-out to Misaki Niigata and Shiori Hosokawa for their ongoing enthusiasm and support.

I would like to thank Saras Sarasvathy, Stuart Read, Yasuhiro Yamakawa, Heidi Neck, Christoph Winkler, Doan Winkel, and Diana Kander for the contributions they have made not only to my life, but also to the field of entrepreneurship. Thank you also to my colleagues in Sweden, Boo Edgar, Karen Williams-Middleton, and Mats Lundqvist, and in Nagano, Sunao Hiruta and Hiroyuki Muramatsu.

I would never have finished this book without my editors, Karina Agbisit and Alan Zatkow. I learned so many new things from both of you. I always felt so much better after our calls. I appreciate Juliette Jarabek's thorough copy editing, Gjorgji Pejkovski and Milan Krstevski for their brilliant work in designing the cover. Brian Bies, your commitment to getting us all published is greatly appreciated. Thank you to Brian's dad, Robert, for providing the initial spark that started the sequence of events that led to this book.

Rym Ali, your sweet e-mails and words of encouragement meant a tremendous amount to me during my moments of doubt.

Thank you to Akiko Gono, who has been a personal mentor to me ever since I interned at the company she founded, Bilingual Group. Your integrity, kindness, and commitment to helping others keeps inspiring me year after year.

And although you are no longer with us, Doris Drucker, I aspire to be like you by enjoying life to the fullest. I have a newspaper article about you playing tennis posted on my door. I have taken up the sport again and am loving it.

To my parents, Satoshi and Keiko Matsuda, I thank you for trusting me in everything I do, and giving me the freedom to pursue the life that I have chosen for myself. I am grateful to Yukiko Makino for the love she shares with me every time I see her, and to Rie and Yoshitaka Mori for taking care of our eldest in Tokyo. To my children, Karen, Akira, and Maya, I thank you for bringing so much joy into my life.

Above all, I would like to thank my husband Yo. I am nothing without you. I can't think of anyone else I would rather be with, so here's to many more years together.

I am humbled and honored for the outpouring of support I received along the way. A special thank-you to everyone who: gave me their time for a personal interview; pre-ordered the e-book, paperback, and multiple copies to make publishing possible; helped spread the word about *Innovation Makers* to build momentum; and gave precious feedback on the manuscript. I am sincerely grateful for all of your help. I would like to acknowledge them one by one (in alphabetical order):

Rym Ali	Michiko Ashizawa
Jack Bergstrand	Ariel Blair
Holly Blondin	Nicholas Cain
Andrew Chen	Jane Chen
May Yee Chen	Michael Cusumano
Mark Dust	Boo Edgar
Kazme Egawa	Yilmaz Emrah Ozden
Nozomi Enomoto	Robert Evans
Zachary First	Thomas Fuhrmann
Michi Fukushima	Naomi Fuwa Fujikawa
Osman Gani	Seiichiro Hangai
Katsuya Hasegawa	Takashi Hasunuma
Hitotora Higashikuni	Nami Hijikata
Sunao Hiruta	Shiori Hosokawa
Joseph Hui	Yasuhiro Ikeuchi
Masao Ishihara	Shonosuke Ishiwatari
Toru Izumoi	Tomoko Kaichi

Diana Kander

Tomoyo Kazumi

Osamu Kikima

Yoshito Koga

Masahiro Kotosaka

Hideo Kudo

William Lee

Yeongjoo Lim

Masahiro Matsuura

Jonathen Morawski

Masanori Nakagawa

Arun Natesan Mangalam

Koji Ogura

Masakatsu Ono

Mitsuo Otohata

Jesse Paliotto

Rob Perhamus

Sven Post

Stuart Read

Bruce Rosenstein

Saras Sarasvathy

Tomoko Saso

Joshua Schare

Dennis Schoeneborn

Cindy Sherman

Hiroko Shiozaki

Mieko Tachikawa

Shozo Takata

Pui-Wing Tam

Hirofumi Taniguchi

Jun Tsusaka

Yuichi Katayori

Sameera Khan

Eric Koester

Shubert Koong

Masaya Kudaka

Joseph Lee

Thomas Liebetruth

Katsufumi Matsui

Mako Miyatake

Frank Moss

Shigeru Nakane

Josephine Nelson

Mariko Omori

Organonmix

Kazuhito Oyobe

Manesh Patel

Goh Wee Ping

Jennifer Rachford

Amy Reynolds

Jay Ross

Makoto Sarata

Shingo Sato

Jeffrey Schnack

Nobuhiro Seki

Toshinari Shimokawa

Junko Suzuki

Susumu Takase

Masaki Takeuchi

Hironobu Tamaki

Mai Trinh

Chikao Ueno

Takaaki Umada

Shengfu Wang

Morio Watanabe

Glen B. Wheatley

Hiromi Yamada

Satoka Yamane

Noriyoshi Yanase

Toshiyuki Yasui

Mari Yoshida

Marissa Ventura

Mariko Watanabe

Lori Weber

Christoph Winkler

Jin-ichiro Yamada

Hideki Yamawaki

Kazuo Yano

Ryota Yokoiwa

Rick Zednick

APPENDIX

INTRODUCTION

Anderson, Chris. Makers: The New Industrial Revolution. New York: Crown Business, 2014. Kindle.

Chen, Danfang, Steffen Heyer, Suphunnika Ibbotson, Konstantinos Salonitis, Jón Garðar Steingrímsson, and Sebastian Thiede. "Direct Digital Manufacturing: Definition, Evolution, and Sustainability Implications." Journal of Cleaner Production 107 (2015): 615-25. https://doi.org/https://doi.org/10.1016/j.jclepro.2015.05.009.

Drucker, Doris. Invent Radium or I'll Pull Your Hair. Chicago: University of Chicago Press, 2004.

Drucker, Peter F. "The Future That Has Already Happened." Harvard Business Review, September-October 1997. https://hbr.org/1997/09/looking-ahead-implications-of-the-present.

Microsoft Imagine. "2020 World Finalists." Imagine Cup website. Accessed September 2, 2020. https://imaginecup.microsoft. com/en-us/Winner/Index/2020WorldChampions.

Miyateu, "日本経済新聞の新聞発行部数推移を50年間分まとめてみた【1970年から2020年】(50 Years' Worth of Nikkei Shimbun Circulation Data (1970-2020))," 新聞についてまとめてみた, May 17, 2020. https://www.otokunamiyateu.com/ entry/newspaper-nikkei.

Mizuho Information and Research Institute, Inc. 平成３０年度創業・起業支援事業（起業家精神に関する調査）(FY2018 Report on Entrepreneurial Spirit Survey). Tokyo: METI, March 2019. https://www.meti.go.jp/meti_lib/report/H30FY/000149. pdf.

Obe, Mitsuru. "Japan GDP Contracts Annualized 27.8% in April-June." Nikkei Asian Review, August 17, 2020. https://asia.nikkei. com/Economy/Japan-GDP-contracts-annualized-27.8-in-April-June.

Valuate Reports. "3D Printing (Additive Manufacturing) Market Size Is Expected to Reach USD 44520 Million by 2026 at a CAGR 31.4%." PR Newswire, March 16, 2020. https://www. prnewswire.com/news-releases/3d-printing-additive-manufacturing-market-size-is-expected-to-reach-usd-44520-million-by-2026—at-a-cagr-31-4—valuates-reports-301024821. html.

Savich, Gleb. "Embrace Infant Warmers Help Save Lives of Preterm Babies in Developing Countries." Medium.com, December 8, 2017. https://medium.com/innovate4health/embrace-infant-

warmers-help-save-lives-of-preterm-babies-in-developing-
countries-bf3fd45cb193.

Yamakawa, Yasuhiro, Mike W. Peng, and David L. Deeds. "Rising
from the Ashes: Cognitive Determinants of Venture Growth
after Entrepreneurial Failure." Entrepreneurship Theory
and Practice 39, no. 2 (2015): 209-36. https://doi.org/10.1111/
etap.12047.

Zernike, Kate. "A New Jersey Township Mourns Yogi Berra, Its
Civic Treasure." The New York Times, September 23, 2015.
https://www.nytimes.com/2015/09/24/nyregion/a-new-jersey-
township-mourns-yogi-its-civic-treasure.html.

CHAPTER 1

Anderson, Chris. "In the Next Industrial Revolution, Atoms Are
the New Bits." Wired.com, January 25, 2010. https://www.wired.
com/2010/01/ff_newrevolution/.

Anderson, Chris. Makers: The New Industrial Revolution. New
York: Crown Business, 2014. Kindle.

Blakemore, Erin. "Youth in Revolt: Five Powerful Movements
Fueled by Young Activists." National Geographic.com, March
23, 2018. https://www.nationalgeographic.com/news/2018/03/
youth-activism-young-protesters-historic-movements/.

Drucker, Peter F. Innovation and Entrepreneurship: Practice and
Principles. New York: Harper & Row, 1985. Kindle.

Drucker, Peter F. Post-Capitalist Society. New York: HarperBusiness, 1993.

Embrace Innovations. "About Us." Accessed August 29, 2020. https://www.embraceinnovations.com/#about-us.

Encyclopaedia Britannica Online. s.v. "Peter F. Drucker: American Economist and Author." Accessed August 29, 2020. https://www.britannica.com/biography/Peter-F-Drucker.

Hatch, Mark. The Maker Movement Manifesto: Rules for Innovation in the New World of Crafters, Hackers, and Tinkerers. New York: McGraw-Hill Education, 2013. Kindle.

Marx, Karl, "German Ideology," Karl Marx Quotes, 1845, https://www.marxists.org/archive/marx/works/subject/quotes/index.htm#:~:text=The%20class%20which%20has%20the,production%20are%20subject%20to%20it.

Stanford University. "Embrace." Design for Extreme Affordability website. Accessed August 29, 2020. https://extreme.stanford.edu/projects/embrace/.

Stanford University. "Stanford d.School" Accessed August 29, 2020, https://dschool.stanford.edu/.

CHAPTER 2

Dictionary.com. s.v. "skunk works." Accessed September 9, 2020. https://www.dictionary.com/browse/skunk-works.

Drucker, Peter F. Innovation and Entrepreneurship: Practice and Principles. New York: Harper & Row, 1985. Kindle.

The Economist. "Skunkworks." The Economist, August 25, 2008. https://www.economist.com/news/2008/08/25/skunkworks.

Lawn, Joshua. "風光変動を再現できる新型回転風洞の開発 Development of a Novel Rotating Wind Tunnel for Reproducing Fluctuations in Wind Direction." Challenge and Creation (C&C) Project 2013 Report. Robert T. Huang Entrepreneurship Center of Kyushu University, 2014.

Mezrich, Ben. The Accidental Billionaires: The Founding of Facebook, a Tale of Sex, Money, Genius and Betrayal. New York: Anchor Books, 2010.

Slywotzky, Adrian. "The Real Secret of Kindle's Success." Fast Company, September 26, 2011. https://www.fastcompany.com/1781303/real-secret-kindles-success.

CHAPTER 3

Amazon. カロリーメイトホルダー（ホワイト）(Calorie Mate Holder (White)." Amazon website, accessed September 7, 2020, https://www.amazon.co.jp/dp/B071J3T8XT/ref=cm_sw_r_tw_dp_x_qhIkzb7F9FKoH.

Berlin, Leslie. Troublemakers: Silicon Valley's Coming of Age. New York: Simon & Schuster, 2017.

Chen, Karin. Techshop: A Case Study in Work Environment Design. (Deloitte University Press, 2013).

Tokyo Metropolitan Government. "新型コロナウイルスに関連した患者の発生について（第52報）(Number of Patients Related to the New Corona Virus (Bulletin No. 52))." News Release, March 1, 2020. https://www.metro.tokyo.lg.jp/tosei/hodohappyo/press/2020/03/01/01.html.

Johnson, Weldon B. "Chandler Techshop Aims to Bring Ideas to Life." The Republic, November 15, 2013.

TechShop. "TechShop CEO Mark Hatch Resigning Position to Pursue Other Opportunities." Global Newswire, July 18, 2016. https://www.globenewswire.com/news-release/2016/07/18/1130558/0/en/TechShop-CEO-Mark-Hatch-Resigning-Position-to-Pursue-Other-Opportunities.html.

Wong, Kenneth. "The End of Techshop: A Huge Loss to the Makers and DIY Community." Digital Engineering 247, November 21, 2017.

Woods, Dan. "Techshop Closes Doors, Files Bankruptcy." Makezine, November 15, 2017. https://makezine.com/2017/11/15/techshop-closes-doors-files-bankruptcy/.

Yokoiwa, Ryota. "カロリーメイト専用ホルダーをamazonで販売しています." 1101001000, Accessed September 7, 2020. https://www.1101001000.com/caloriemateholder.

CHAPTER 4

Arend, Richard J., Hessamoddin Sarooghi, and Andrew Burkemper. "Effectuation as Ineffectual? Applying the 3e Theory-Assessment Framework to a Proposed New Theory of Entrepreneurship." Academy of Management Review 40, no. 4 (2015): 630-51. https://doi.org/10.5465/amr.2014.0455.

Aydin, Rebecca. "How 3 Guys Turned Renting Air Mattresses in Their Apartment into a $31 Billion Company, Airbnb." Business Insider, September 20, 2019. https://www.businessinsider.com/how-airbnb-was-founded-a-visual-history-2016-2.

Buchanan, Leigh. "How Great Entrepreneurs Think." Inc., February 1, 2011. https://www.inc.com/magazine/20110201/how-great-entrepreneurs-think.html.

Colker, David. "Doris Drucker Dies at 103; Memoirist and Wife of Peter Drucker." Los Angeles Times, October 4 2014. https://www.latimes.com/local/obituaries/la-me-doris-drucker-20141005-story.html.

Drucker, Peter F. Innovation and Entrepreneurship: Practice and Principles. New York: Harper & Row, 1985. Kindle.

Effectuation.org. What Is Effectuation? The Rector and Visitors of the University of Virginia, 2011 Accessed September 20, 2020. https://www.effectuation.org/sites/default/files/documents/effectuation-3-pager.pdf.

Encylopaedia Britannica Online. s.v. "Herbert A. Simon: American Social Scientist." Accessed September 13, 2020. https://www.britannica.com/biography/Herbert-A-Simon.

Jasper. "The Airbnb Founder Story: From Selling Cereals to a $25B Company," Get Paid for Your Pad, August 8, 2019. https://get-paidforyourpad.com/blog/the-airbnb-founder-story/.

Katz, Jerome. "The Chronology and Intellectual Trajectory of American Entrepreneurship Education 1876-1999." Journal of Business Venturing 18 (2003): 283-300. https://doi.org/doi:10.1016/S0883-9026(02)00098-8.

Kitching, John, and Julia Rouse. "Contesting Effectuation Theory: Why It Does Not Explain New Venture Creation." International Small Business Journal, (February 2020). https://doi.org/10.1177/0266242620904638.

Knowledge@Wharton, "The Inside Story Behind the Unlikely Rise of Airbnb," Knowledge@Wharton, April 26, 2017, https://knowledge.wharton.upenn.edu/article/the-inside-story-behind-the-unlikely-rise-of-airbnb/.

Merriam-Webster. s.v. "effectuate (verb)." Accessed September 13, 2020, https://www.merriam-webster.com/dictionary/effectuate.

Mizuho Information and Research Institute, Inc. 平成３０年度創業・起業支援事業（起業家精神に関する調査）(FY2018 Report on Entrepreneurial Spirit). Tokyo: METI, March 2019. https://www.meti.go.jp/meti_lib/report/H30FY/000149.pdf.

Patil, Rashmi. "Like Science, Even Entrepreneurship Should Be Taught at the School Level: Darden Prof Saras D Sarasvathy." Edex Live, July 27, 2019. https://www.edexlive.com/people/2019/jul/27/how-darden-prof-saras-d-sarasvathy-used-effectuation-to-understand-entrepreneurship-7211.html.

Read, Stuart, Saras D. Sarasvathy, Nick Dew, and Robert Wiltbank. Effectual Entrepreneurship. London and New York: Routledge/Taylor & Francis Group, 2017.

Sarasvathy, D.K., Herbert A. Simon, and Lester Lave. "Perceiving and Managing Business Risks: Differences between Entrepreneurs and Bankers." Journal of Economic Behavior & Organization 33, no. 2 (1998): 207-25. https://doi.org/https://doi.org/10.1016/S0167-2681(97)00092-9.

Sarasvathy, Saras D. "Causation and Effectuation: Toward a Theoretical Shift from Economic Inevitability to Entrepreneurial Contingency." Academy of Management Review 26, no. 2 (2001): 243-63. https://doi.org/10.5465/AMR.2001.4378020.

Sarasvathy, Saras D. Effectuation: Elements of Entrepreneurial Expertise. New Horizons in Entrepreneurship. Cheltenham; Northampton: Edward Elgar, 2008.

USASBE. "Bill Aulet on "What I've Learned About Teaching Entrepreneurship"." Medium.com, April 8, 2019. https://medium.com/@USASBE/bill-aulet-on-what-ive-learned-about-teaching-entrepreneurship-395117694e11.

Yoffie, David B., and Michael A. Cusumano. Strategy Rules : Five Timeless Lessons from Bill Gates, Andy Grove, and Steve Jobs. New York: HarperBusiness, 2015.

CHAPTER 5

Berlin, Leslie. Troublemakers: Silicon Valley's Coming of Age. New York: Simon & Schuster, 2017.

Blank, Steve, "The Startup Team," Steve Blank (blog), December 13, 2011. https://steveblank.com/2011/12/13/the-startup-team/.

Colao, J.J. "Steve Blank Introduces Scientists to a New Variable: Customers." Forbes, August 1, 2012. https://www.forbes.com/sites/jjcolao/2012/08/01/steve-blank-introduces-scientists-to-a-new-variable-customers/#3d19d8759b4c.

Constable, Giff. Talking to Humans: Success Starts with Understanding Your Customers. Giff Constable, 2014.

Drucker, Peter F., and Joseph A. Maciariello. Management. New York: Collins, 2008.

Ginreikai. "Ginreikai Home." Accessed September 28, 2020. https://www.ginreikai.net/.

Lohr, Steve. "The Rise of the Fleet-Footed Startup." The New York Times, April 24, 2010. https://www.nytimes.com/2010/04/25/business/25unboxed.html.

Ochi, Gakuto. "【2019年版】日本のファブ施設調査——調査開始後、初の減少 2018年比15％減([2019] Japan's Fab Facilities Decline for the First Time since Survey Start: Down 15% vs 2018)" Fabcross.com, December 23, 2019. https://fabcross.jp/topics/research/20181223_fabspace.html.

Ries, Eric. The Lean Startup: How Today's Entrepreneurs Use Continuous Innovation to Create Radically Successful Businesses. New York: Crown Business, 2011.

Wagner, Tony, and Robert A. Compton. Creating Innovators: The Making of Young People Who Will Change the World. New York: Scribner, 2012.

Yujie, Xue. "Made in China: The Boom and Bust of Makerspaces."
Sixth Tone, November 8, 2018. https://www.sixthtone.com/
news/1003171/made-in-china-the-boom-and-bust-of-maker-
spaces.

CHAPTER 6

Amabile, Teresa, and Steven j. Kramer. "The Power of Small Wins."
Harvard Business Review, May 2011. https://hbr.org/2011/05/
the-power-of-small-wins.

Clarey, Christopher. "Olympians Use Imagery as Mental Training." The New York Times, February 22, 2014. https://www.
nytimes.com/2014/02/23/sports/olympics/olympians-use-im-
agery-as-mental-training.html.

Connected Robotics. "Connected Robotics." Accessed September
21, 2020. https://connected-robotics.com/en/.

Cooperrider, David L., and Diana Kaplin Whitney. Appreciative
Inquiry: A Positive Revolution in Change. San Francisco, CA:
Berrett-Koehler, 2005.

Fredrickson, Barbara L. "What Good Are Positive Emotions?".
Review of General Psychology 2, no. 3 (1998): 300-19.

Gielnik, Michael, Matthias Spitzmuller, Antje Schmitt, D. Katha-
rina Klemann, and Michael Frese. ""I Put in Effort, Therefore I
Am Passionate": Investigating the Path from Effort to Passion
in Entrepreneurship." Academy of Management Journal 58, no.
4 (2015): 1-42. https://doi.org/10.5465/amj.2011.0727.

Ishii, Ryo. "ソフトとハードを自在に！目指すは”欲しい”が作れる
エンジニア (Moving Freely between Software and Hardware!
Aspiration to Become an Engineer Who Can Build "Wants")."
EMIRA, June 26, 2018. https://emira-t.jp/rikei/6587/.

Ishii, Ryo. "自動調理ロボットを作りたい理系女子！あの映画み
たいに朝の時間を快適にしたい (A Woman in STEM Hopes
to Make a Cooking Robot! Craving Mornings Like the One
in the Movies)." EMIRA, June 26, 2018. https://emira-t.jp/
rikei/6573/.

Makino, Emi. "Appreciative Inquiry Summits and Organizational
Knowledge Creation: A Social Systems Perspective." PhD diss.,
Claremont Graduate University, 2013.

Miyatake, Mako, "最適化わたあめ(Optimized Cotton Candy)."
Mako Miyatake Portfolio, October, 2018, https://www.makomi-
yatake.com/project-03.

SXSW. "About SXSW." Accessed September 22, 2020. https://www.
sxsw.com/about/.

Tamesue, Dai. Winning Alone. Tokyo: President, 2020.

Toth, Andy. "You Should Read This before Starting a Company."
Medium.com, November 2, 2015. https://medium.com/@
toth/you-should-read-this-before-starting-a-company-
b15d0885b30f.

Zemeckis, Robert, dir. Back to the Future. 1985; Universal Pictures.

CHAPTER 7

Chen, Jane. "Embrace the Entrepreneurial Journey." Entrepreneurial Thought Leaders, Stanford eCorner, October 26, 2016. https://ecorner.stanford.edu/videos/embrace-the-entrepreneurial-journey/.

Csikszentmihalyi, Mihaly. Finding Flow: The Psychology of Engagement with Everyday Life. Masterminds. New York: BasicBooks, 1997.

Csikszentmihalyi, Mihaly. Flow: The Psychology of Optimal Experience. New York: Harper & Row, 1990.

Ericsson, K. Anders. "Deliberate Practice and Acquisition of Expert Performance: A General Overview." Academic Emergency Medicine 15, no. 11 (2008): 988-94.

Information-technology Promotion Agency. "MITOU Program." Accessed October 13, 2020. https://www.ipa.go.jp/english/humandev/third.html.

Muramatsu, Kotaro. "Todai to Texas ユニークな発想と技術で世界に挑戦." Todai Shimbun Online, March 20, 2019. https://www.todaishimbun.org/todai-to-texas20190320/.

Neck, Heidi M., Patricia G. Greene, and Candida G. Brush. Teaching Entrepreneurship: A Practice-Based Approach. Cheltenham; Northampton: Edward Elgar, 2014.

Rigney, Ryan. "A Game Design Legend Revisits His Theory of Fun." Wired, November 18, 2013. https://www.wired.com/2013/11/theory-of-fun-revised/.

UNICEF. "Convention on the Rights of the Child Text." Accessed October 13, 2020, https://www.unicef.org/child-rights-convention/convention-text.

Wagner, Tony, and Robert A. Compton. Creating Innovators: The Making of Young People Who Will Change the World. New York: Scribner, 2012.

Westbrook, Andrew, and Todd S. Braver. "Dopamine Does Double Duty in Motivating Cognitive Effort." Neuron 89, no. 4 (2016): 695-710. https://doi.org/10.1016/j.neuron.2015.12.029.

CHAPTER 8

Brown, Michael E., and Linda K. Treviño. "Do Role Models Matter? An Investigation of Role Modeling as an Antecedent of Perceived Ethical Leadership." Journal of Business Ethics 122, no. 4 (2014): 587-98. https://doi.org/10.1007/s10551-013-1769-0.

Davis, Jeffrey. "How Creativity Builds Resilience in Times of Crisis." Psychology Today, June 16, 2020. https://www.psychologytoday.com/us/blog/tracking-wonder/202006/how-creativity-builds-resilience-in-times-crisis.

Sarasvathy, Saras D. "Causation and Effectuation: Toward a Theoretical Shift from Economic Inevitability to Entrepreneurial Contingency." Academy of Management Review 26, no. 2 (2001): 243-63. https://doi.org/10.5465/AMR.2001.4378020.

Sharp. "ヘルシオホットクック[Healsio Hotcook]." Accessed October 13, 2020, https://jp.sharp/hotcook/.

CHAPTER 9

Bass, Bernard M., and Ronald E. Riggio. Transformational Leadership. Mahwah, N.J.: L. Erlbaum Associates, 2006.

Biz/Zine. "執筆者情報 馬田 隆明 (Author Information Takaaki Umada)." Biz/Zine. Accessed October 13, 2020. https://bizzine.jp/person/detail/237.

Christensen, Clayton M., Michael E. Raynor, and Rory McDonald. "What Is Disruptive Innovation?" Harvard Business Review, December 2015. https://hbr.org/2015/12/what-is-disruptive-innovation.

Business Dictionary. s.v. "Transformational Leadership." Accessed October 13, 2020. http://www.businessdictionary.com/definition/transformational-leadership.html.

FastGrow. "馬田 隆明 [Umada Takaaki]." FastGrow, June 28, 2019, Accessed October 13, 2020. https://www.fastgrow.jp/people/953.

Graham, Paul, "How Y Combinator Started," March, 2012, http://www.paulgraham.com/ycstart.html.

Graham, Paul, Jessica Livingston, Robert Morris, and Trevor Blackwell, "Y Combinator's Founding Principles," October, 2017.

Hasegawa, Katsuya. Startups 101. Tokyo: University of Tokyo Press, 2019.

Hongo Tech Garage. "Project 募集するプロジェクトについて." Accessed October 13, 2020. https://www.hongotechgarage.com/project/.

Kakouris, Alexandros, and Panagiotis Georgiadis. "Analysing Entrepreneurship Education: A Bibliometric Survey Pattern." [In English]. Journal of Global Entrepreneurship Research 6, no. 1 (Feb 2016): 1-18. https://doi.org/http://dx.doi.org/10.1186/s40497-016-0046-y.

Kumparak, Greg. "These Are the Top Y Combinator Companies of All Time, Based on Valuation." TechCrunch, October 2, 2019. https://techcrunch.com/2019/10/02/these-are-the-top-y-combinator-companies-of-all-time-based-on-valuation/?guccounter=1.

Mantra. "世界のマンガファンにリアルタイムで多言語配信、マンガAI翻訳のMantraが資金調達を実施." PR Times, June 8, 2020. https://prtimes.jp/main/html/rd/p/000000001.000059295.html.

Read, Stuart, Saras D. Sarasvathy, Nick Dew, and Robert Wiltbank. Effectual Entrepreneurship. London and New York: Routledge/Taylor & Francis Group, 2017.

Ries, Eric. The Lean Startup: How Today's Entrepreneurs Use Continuous Innovation to Create Radically Successful Businesses. New York: Crown Business, 2011.

Schumpeter, Joseph. Theory of Economic Development. Routledge, 2017.

Shontell, Alyson. "Paul Graham Founded Y Combinator 7 Years Ago to Create a Job for His Wife." Business Insider, March 18, 2012. https://www.businessinsider.com/how-y-combinator-started-2012-3.

The University of Tokyo, and Daiwa Securities Group Inc. "東京大
　　学と大和証券グループによる産学連携「東京大学本郷テッ
　　クガレージ（大和証券グループ寄附プロジェクト）」を設置."
　　News Release, September 9, 2016. https://www.ducr.u-tokyo.
　　ac.jp/content/400059641.pdf.

Y Combinator. "Jessica Livingston on the Accidental Origin of
　　Y Combinator," November 25, 2015. https://blog.ycombinator.
　　com/jessica-livingston-startup-school-radio/.

EPILOGUE

Foo, Audrey. "5 Scary Japanese Foods and Why You Should Try
　　Them." Japan Today, August 19, 2018. https://japantoday.com/
　　category/features/food/5-scary-japanese-foods-and-why-you-
　　should-try-them.

Jobs, Steve. ""You've Got to Find What You Love," Jobs Says."
　　Stanford News, 2005. https://news.stanford.edu/2005/06/14/
　　jobs-061505/.

Zernike, Kate. "A New Jersey Township Mourns Yogi Berra, Its
　　Civic Treasure." The New York Times, September 23, 2015.
　　https://www.nytimes.com/2015/09/24/nyregion/a-new-jersey-
　　township-mourns-yogi-its-civic-treasure.html.